*1. Seek His Face*

# SEEK HIS FACE

# Short meditations for Sundays and some feas

# SEEK HIS FACE

ays, based on readings from the Lectionary

by Brother Anthony J. Pfarr, S.J.

*Imprimi potest:*
Robert F. Harvanek, S.J.
Provincial, Chicago Province

*Nihil Obstat:*
Rev. Alfred J. Connick, J.C.D.

*Imprimatur:*
✠ Humberto S. Medeiros
Archbishop of Boston

May 29, 1973

## *Acknowledgements*

The text of the *New American Bible*, copyright © 1970 by the Confraternity of Christian Doctrine, Washington, D.C. (Books 1 Samuel to 2 Maccabees, 1969) is reproduced herein by license of said Confraternity of Christian Doctrine. All rights reserved.

Excerpts from *Documents of Vatican II, in a New and Definitive Translation*, Walter Abbott, ed., are reprinted with permission from *America* (1966). All rights reserved. © 1966. America Press, Inc., 106 West 56th Street, New York, N.Y. 10019.

Entrance and Communion antiphons and excerpts from sequences reprinted with permission of Bishops' Committee on the Liturgy.

English translation of selected responsorial antiphons and gospel acclamations from the Lectionary
Copyright © 1969, International Committee on English in the Liturgy, Inc. All rights reserved.

Two Opening Prayers reprinted from *The Maryknoll Missal* (Vatican II Edition), edited by the Maryknoll Fathers, copyright © 1966 by P.J. Kenedy and Sons. Used with permission.
The "O" Antiphons (Fourth Sunday of Advent), from *The Hours of the Divine Office*, Vol. I, published by The Liturgical Press. Copyrighted by The Order of St. Benedict, Inc., Collegeville, Minnesota. Used with permission.

Other acknowledgements appear in text or footnotes.

The occasional verses are the author's.

Although it is impossible to recall all the sources and to give specific credit, the author is also indebted to retreat directors, spiritual advisers and no doubt to other authors for a considerable number of the ideas developed in these meditations.

Library of Congress Catalog Card Number 73–86211



*Printed in U.S.A. by the Daughters of St. Paul*
*50 St. Paul's Ave., Boston, Ma. 02130*

*The Daughters of St. Paul are*
*an international religious congregation*
*serving the Church with the communications*
*media.*

## Dedication

*To the devoted Men of Bellarmine*
*on their Silver Jubilee*
*1948-1973*

## List of Abbreviations used in this book (as in the **New American Bible**)

|  |  |
|---|---|
| Genesis | Gn. |
| Exodus | Ex. |
| Leviticus | Lv. |
| Numbers | Nm. |
| Deuteronomy | Dt. |
| Joshua | Jos. |
| 1 Kings | 1 Kgs. |
| Judith | Jdt. |
| Job | Jb. |
| Psalms | Ps. |
| Proverbs | Prv. |
| Ecclesiastes | Eccl. |
| Song of Songs | Sg. |
| Wisdom | Wis. |
| Sirach (Ecclesiasticus) | Sir. |
| Isaiah | Is. |
| Jeremiah | Jer. |
| Lamentations | Lam. |
| Ezekiel | Ez. |
| Daniel | Dn. |
| Hosea | Hos. |
| Jonah | Jon. |
| Zephaniah | Zep. |
| Haggai | Hg. |
| Zechariah | Zec. |
| Malachi | Mal. |
| Matthew | Mt. |
| Mark | Mk. |
| Luke | Lk. |
| John | Jn. |
| Acts of the Apostles | Acts |
| Romans | Rom. |
| 1 Corinthians | 1 Cor. |
| 2 Corinthians | 2 Cor. |
| Galatians | Gal. |
| Ephesians | Eph. |
| Philippians | Phil. |
| Colossians | Col. |
| 1 Thessalonians | 1 Thes. |
| 2 Thessalonians | 2 Thes. |
| 1 Timothy | 1 Tm. |
| 2 Timothy | 2 Tm. |
| Hebrews | Heb. |
| James | Jas. |
| 1 Peter | 1 Pt. |
| 2 Peter | 2 Pt. |
| 1 John | 1 Jn. |
| Revelation | Rv. |

## CONTENTS

# Foreword

The author presents these meditations with some misgivings, hoping simply that they will encourage meditation on the Sacred Scriptures, and especially on those passages that have been selected for the *Lectionary* to make our liturgical celebrations more meaningful and joyful. Usually the readings for a given Sunday are in some way related, throwing light one on the other or reinforcing a theme. If what is presented here helps some to pray, it will be the work of the Holy Spirit through the revealed word of God rather than anything the author may have added.

The readings for Mass, recently revised to present to us a much larger and richer selection of the Sacred Scriptures, are meant to help us toward that more intelligent and more responsive participation which the Second Vatican Council asks of us. Every instructed Catholic knows what the Eucharistic Sacrifice is essentially, but it is good to hear it again from the sacred council. It returns to this sacrifice and sacrament repeatedly, especially in the documents on the liturgy, on bishops, on priests, and on the laity.

> The Lord's sacrifice is offered in the Eucharist in a sacramental manner, in memory of Him until He returns. It perpetuates the sacrifice of the cross throughout the centuries, making present to us the victory and triumph of His death. For us Christ offered to the Father, and now bids us offer, the sacrifice of His body and blood.

It is a sacrament of love and sign of unity. It is a memorial of the Lord's death *and resurrection,* and so we celebrate it joyfully.
Priests are to consider that they fulfill their chief duty in the mystery of the Eucharist; and they should arrange for this Sacrifice to be the center and culmination of the whole life of the Christian community.
The laity are reminded that the sacraments, and especially the Eucharist, communicate the charity which is the soul of all apostolic work.
Our Mass consists of two parts, the Liturgy of the Word and the Liturgy of the Eucharist, making together one single act of worship. In it we are instructed by God's word and refreshed at the Lord's table.

The *Lectionary* provides three readings for Sundays and some feasts, and the texts for these are arranged in a three-year cycle, designated A, B and C. Thus the readings are repeated only every fourth year, i.e., 1973 is Year B, 1974 is Year C, 1975 is Year A, etc. In this book, at the top of the page beginning each meditation, along with the texts suggested for reading before prayer, is given the cycle on which the considerations are based. The majority draw upon the readings of cycle B, but some on a combination of cycles, and a very few exclusively on cycle A or C.

That these short meditations may be useful independently of a particular day's readings from the Lectionary, an index by general topic has been added.

It is recommended that the suggested texts be read beforehand even though in some cases a considerable part of them appears within the meditation. It may be that this previous Scripture reading, if done reflectively, will be enough to fill the time of prayer. The insights and spiritual movements that come to one directly through the word of God are the most genuine and satisfying.

It may be helpful to some to recall a few ideas on prayer:

1) I give God a chance to speak to me by disengaging my mind from the thoughts and cares that fill busy days, finding a place of silence—at least within the mind and heart. It is possible to pray anywhere, but it requires effort and practice to retire to the silent oratory within me; or to withdraw momentarily from my preoccupation and beam toward heaven a quick signal of desire, praise or gratitude.

2) A certain reverence is necessary. The body may express this in many ways, but interior reverence is the more important. I strive for respectful, exclusive attention to the One with whom I would converse.

3) Prayer is a communicating relationship with God. It includes the relationships of son and Father; of servant and Lord; of creature and Creator; of friend or disciple and Christ; of lovers.

4) Prayer should become spontaneous, so I must pray in a way suitable to myself: according to my character and present disposition, my faith and understanding, my gift of grace.

5) A very important point of procedure in prayer is that when a point strikes me as a new view or deeper insight, or provides an impulse of the affections toward God—whether of sorrow, desire, admiration, gratitude, love—I do not proceed further. It is possible that such a movement of the spirit may not come in a whole hour of consideration, reading and patient petitioning; or it may come after only a moment of consideration, a single phrase of Sacred Scripture.

It is this movement of the heart that I search for, and when it is given I should not push on to other ideas.

6) I must continue with patience in prayer in the face of apparent failure or futility. It is for God to give, when He pleases, any light to the mind or joy to the spirit. At times He may leave me in a state of dullness and immobility; but, if I continue with humility and trust, there will be a time of clearer understanding, firmer hope and greater joy; a time of love that is proven and deepened by previous apparent withdrawal.

Come, Holy Spirit, fill the hearts
of Your faithful, kindle in them
the fire of Your love!

## A Preparatory Prayer

(Psalm 27:7-9)

Hear, O Lord, the sound of my call;
have pity on me, and answer me.
Of you my heart speaks; you my
  glance seeks;
your presence, O Lord, I seek.
Hide not your face from me;
do not in anger repel your servant.
You are my helper: cast me not off;
forsake me not, O God my savior.

## Hear my call!

We trust that You do. Being ignored, even the fear of being ignored, is anguish. But You, God, are Father, we, Your children. You do not turn away.

## Pity me!

See my need! As creature, broken by sin, I am wretchedly poor, and blind, and naked.

Empty, I come begging from You, fullness of being, the All.

Shortsighted, ignorant and confused, I look to You, the all-seeing, the all-knowing.

My shortcomings laid bare, I ask to be clothed in Your integrity, Your grace.

## Answer me!

Not so much "Give this to me," but show that You hear—that You know and care.

## My heart speaks of you; I seek your presence, your face

In silence, the wordless voice wells up from the depths of my being. I am pressed to search for You, to come face to face, to be enthralled by goodness, beauty and love.

## ...your face

Yes, You are *Person:* Father, Friend, Lover.

*Father:* that You are *Father* justifies in me what might otherwise be brashness, presumption, exasperating persistence.

*Jesus:* let my prayer to You be open communication with the perfect Friend; face-to-face interchange, without embarrassment of slight acquaintance, uneasiness of imperfect trust, and defensive reservations.

*Holy Spirit:* take possession of my heart, as Love, so that there may be union of desire and will. And may there be overflow of love: outpouring as of a river seeking out and trying to fill all the deep hollows of human need.

First Sunday of Advent

Read Rom. 13:11-14
Mk. 13:33-37
(B, A)

# I The Night Is Far Spent

> *...It is now the hour for you to wake from sleep.... The night is far spent; the day draws near.*[1]
> *...come,*
> *let us walk in the light of the Lord.*[2]

The season of Advent is the dawning of the light of Christ. The liturgy spans the whole pre-Christian and Christian eras, preparing us for Christ's first coming, as a child; and His last, in great power, to judge.

Advent is a time of quickening hope, of desire. It summarizes and ends the long, dark centuries before Christ when moral corruption spread with the human race throughout the world. St. Paul describes the men who so much needed redemption:

> *...filled with every kind of wickedness: maliciousness, greed, ill will, envy, murder, bickering, deceit, craftiness...slanderers, they hate God, are insolent, haughty, boastful, ingenious in their wrong-doing and rebellious toward their parents.*[3]

These included the Romans, acknowledged as leaders of their world in art and architecture, administration and law, military prowess. Masters of the political world—but not of their souls. This is unredeemed man.

God's chosen race also needed to acknowledge its share in the universal corruption, so often recalled to it by the prophets.

*...Behold, you are angry, and we are sinful....*[4]

## II Stay Awake!

We can be as men still sleeping in the darkness that Christ came to dispel. It is imperative that we rise from indifference and lethargy that are induced by weak faith and total involvement in a world at odds with Christ. A response, a radical choice, is demanded of every man who meets Christ.

*What is your opinion about the Messiah?*[5]

No other question the human tongue can form is as vitally important, as urgent, as this.

When later the child Christ will be carried into the temple to be presented to the Lord, the old man Simeon will say of Him that He is set as a sign that many will reject. He is the sign of the Father's love for men, and many will reject that love. Our response to love, a day-by-day response, must prepare us for His final coming.

*Be constantly on the watch! Stay awake!*[6]

## III Seek Justice

We find this word "justice" frequently in the Advent liturgy. In other translations the idea was rendered as "righteousness" or "integrity." It is a wholeness, a spiritual soundness, an inner unity of our being in harmony with the will of the Creator. Jesus was to *do what is right and just in the land.* The city of the Lord was to be called, *The Lord-our-justice.*[7]

We long to be whole, perfect in our personality, yet find ourselves divided, caught in a turmoil of contradictions. Paul's eloquence has touched upon this lack of integrity within us.

> *I cannot even understand my own actions. I do not do what I want to do but what I hate... the desire to do right is there but not the power.*[8]

With humility, patience, hope, we seek wholeness.

> *...all of us have become like unclean men,*
> *all our good deeds are like polluted rags;*
> *We have all withered like leaves,*
> *and our guilt carries us away like the wind.*[9]

O Lord, stir up Your might and come![10]

1. Rom. 13:11-12 (second reading, A)
2. Is. 2:5 (first reading, A)
3. Rom. 1:29-30
4. Is. 64:4 (first reading, B)
5. Mt. 22:42
6. Mk. 13:33 (Gospel, B)
7. Jer. 33:15, 16 (first reading, B)
8. Rom. 7:15, 18
9. Is. 64:5
10. Opening prayer

## Second Sunday of Advent

Read Is. 40:1-5, 9-11
2 Pt. 3:8-14
(B)

The first reading, responsorial psalm and Gospel for today (Cycle B) begin with words that express the joyful hope that is the spirit of Advent. They supply three fertile seeds for our contemplation.

### I The Beginning of the Good News[1]

This is Mark's introduction to his Gospel. The substitution of "good news" for "gospel" which has recently become common is a happy change, for most of us are somewhat "listless listeners" and too slow to make the translation in the moment of introduction to the reading.

We may say that liturgically Advent is the beginning of the Good News, which is spelled out and enlarged upon through the rest of the year. With great good news comes the urge to celebrate, and all our repeated liturgical sacrifices are celebrations. Even during Lent, when our joy is subdued by emphasis on our sinfulness and on Christ's sufferings because of it, there is always the underlying joy of firm hope for ourselves and gratitude to the Savior.

A poet has written, "God's in his heaven, all's right with the world!"[2] but this does not carry the full import of the Christian message. God in heaven can seem so remote from man, a Creator who shaped the ball of the earth and tossed it spinning on its own way in the vast darkness below Him. A God inaccessible and indifferent to man, the little creature He has placed on this small spaceship and left subject to vicissitudes which seem blind chance, mindless fate. The kernel of the Good News is that the God of heaven stepped into His world, and by His presence even more than His human words, assures us that He is not remote and indifferent. John, in his version of the Good News, after trying to express the nature of God's Son, gives the reason for the joy of the message he passes on to us: *He was in the world....*[3]

## II Comfort My People[4]

This was the role of the prophets, who play such a large part in the Advent liturgy. They wrote the first large headlines of the Good News, but their story was necessarily skimpy on details. The big story was repeated and continually enlarged upon through centuries, and by the time of Mark's proclamation, and even more so of John's, it was firmly established and well detailed. Isaiah was empowered in God's name to *speak tenderly to Jerusalem.*[5] Jerusalem, the chosen city of God, is now the Church. The message still brings gladness to the hearts of millions. It proclaims the cancellation of sin, the end of a pressing indebtedness, and a new life. The Good News can save those who have substituted "kicks," chemical stimulation, lawless self-fulfillment, for the deep joy and peace which follow conformity to God's plan, a harmonious relationship with all His creation. This has a price; but to refuse to pay anything in terms of self-discipline is to refuse the real happiness offered through the Good News.

## III God Proclaims Peace[6]

Lord God, we will listen. Peace is such a rich word, such a desirable thing, and so often far from us. Peace of heart is an incomparable treasure, and can only come from You. We beg for it. And we ask You to help us prepare for it, for we are constantly urged to prepare a way for the Lord. Jesus, You have come into our world, but You can enter our hearts, with Your peace, only when we are prepared for You; when we have leveled the hills of our pride, self-sufficiency and self-seeking; and filled in the valleys of omission of the many possible acts of kindness and love to our neighbor.

You tell us, Lord God, that righteousness and peace embrace, and that righteousness is from heaven. It is not from ourselves that we expect to be justified, not merely through any exact keeping of Your law, but through the righteousness from heaven, the justification brought down to us by the Word made flesh. With our loving acceptance of Your Son we find peace. This is the joy of Your Good News for us. Make us listen attentively, and thank You with all our hearts.

1. Mk. 1:1
2. Robert Browning, "Pippa Passes"
3. Jn. 1:10
4. Is. 40:1
5. Is. 40:2
6. Ps. 85:9

## Third Sunday of Advent

Read Is. 35:1-6, 10
Jn. 1:6-8, 19-28
Mt. 11:7-11
(B, A, C)

# I Prepare!

*"I am*
*'a voice in the desert, crying out:*
*Make straight the way of the Lord!'"*[1]

As Christmas draws near and we are busied with many preparations, we begin to feel the glow of this unique season. The bright stores, the carols, the jolly Santas, put us in gay spirits. But suddenly, in our liturgy, there falls across our path the shadow of a man up from the hinterland, a gaunt and shaggy figure with the burning eyes of the zealot and rough voice booming above the sound of our bells and music:

*Make ready the way of the Lord,*
*Clear him a straight path.*[2]

But aren't we preparing for the Lord? For His birthday? If John the Baptist seems a threatening shadow on our joyous preparations for Christmas, we might examine them critically. For John *does* come with high credentials. The prophet Malachi told of him,

*Lo, I am sending my messenger*
*to prepare the way before me;*

*And suddenly there will come to the temple the Lord whom you seek....*[3]

And Christ Himself:

*...history has not known a man born of woman greater than John the Baptizer.*[4]

The un-Christian world has adopted Christmas too, but left little of Christ in it. It accepts the accidentals, feasting and gift-giving, decoration and celebration, and also a certain spirit of fellowship and kindness. But Christmas is simply Christ the Redeemer come to save us, asking on our part a *heart* prepared to receive Him. The Baptist insists on this renewal of heart.

*Even now the ax is laid to the root of the tree. Every tree that is not fruitful will be cut down and thrown into the fire.*
*His winnowing-fan is in his hand. He will clear the threshing floor....*[5]

## II What Must We Do?

John gave some specific answers to this. The tax collectors had a reputation for enriching themselves, and so the directive, "Exact nothing over and above your fixed amount." Soldiers are inclined to violence, so, "Don't bully anyone. Denounce no one falsely." And *to all the people*, the universal and all-inclusive law of practical love. In those simple times simple directives sufficed:

*"Let the man with two coats give to the man who has none. The man who has food should do the same."*[6]

In our complex society it may be more difficult to know in detail "what we must do." But even today there are implications for the merchant, the man providing service, the banker, the business profit-planners in the directions, "Exact nothing over and above your fixed amount." Similarly, for those in labor unions and their officials, "Be content with your pay" may at times be a proper decision. There must be at least a justification for demanding an increase, and a consideration of the common good. And there is no escaping the injunction for those who *have* to share with those who *have not.*

> *Test everything; retain what is good. Avoid any semblance of evil. May the God of peace make you perfect in holiness.*[7]

## III Rejoice

In spite of any shadow that the ascetical John might seem to cast upon us, the dominant theme in today's liturgy is joy: Christ is near! He saves, heals, renews! Paul writes to his Thessalonian Christians: *Rejoice always....*[8] And to those of Philippi: *Rejoice in the Lord always! I say it again. Rejoice!*[9]

> *Be glad and exult with all your heart....*
> *The Lord, your God, is in your midst....*
> *He will rejoice over you with gladness*
> *and renew you in his love....*[10]

We rejoice over the great Good News that God comes to our world; that His mighty love is in the heart of a Man, all-embracing, but reaching out especially to the poor, the sorrowing, the burdened.[11]

1. Jn. 1:23 (Gospel, B)
2. Lk. 3:4
3. Mal. 3:1
4. Mt. 11:11 (Gospel, A)
5. Mt. 3:10, 12
6. Lk. 3:11 (Gospel, C)
7. 1 Thes. 5:21-23 (second reading, B)
8. 1 Thes. 5:18
9. Phil. 4:4 (second reading, C)
10. Zep. 3:14, 17 (first reading, C)
11. Cf. Is. 61:1 (first reading, B)

## Fourth Sunday of Advent *

In the Divine Office, beginning on December 17, and running through December 23, we have the "O" antiphons, which are introductory verses for the *Magnificat* said at vespers. They are varied expressions of impassioned appeal for the coming of the Savior, and lend themselves to a simple prayer of the affections in which we dwell upon them, word by word, phrase by phrase, as long as they stir some movement of faith, desire, hope, gratitude, love. The antiphons follow, with short comments, a suggestion of what may be drawn from them.

> (December 17) "O Wisdom, you came forth from the mouth of the Most High, and reaching from beginning to end, you ordered all things mightily and sweetly. Come and teach us the way of prudence!"[1]

Jesus is Wisdom, the Word, Person equal to the Father. *The Word became flesh....*[2] "Out of the mouth of the Most High"—perfect expression of the infinite knowing of God.

"Reaching from end to end...." All the good, beauty, order in the universe, "from end to end," is the work of Wisdom, the Word, together with the Father and the Holy Spirit. *Through him all things came into being....*[3]

* Note: These considerations are not based directly on the readings for this Sunday. For a consideration based on the Gospel, B, see Annunciation, p. 238.

"Come and teach us the way of prudence." *Come!* One syllable epitomizes the Advent liturgy, explodes with all the desires built up through centuries in a suffering humanity made for God but alienated from Him.

> (December 18) "O Adonai and Ruler of the house of Israel, you appeared to Moses in the fire of the burning bush, and on Mount Sinai gave him your law. Come, and with an outstretched arm redeem us!"[4]

"O Adonai"—Lord of lords. "Ruler"—a true leader, knowing the way, never swerving from it through personal passion or weakness. Who "appeared to Moses," to the accompaniment of thunder: come now as a man of meekness and peace, even as a small child. "With an outstretched arm redeem us!" Those short baby arms stretched out for Mary's care, they shall redeem us in the strength of God. Moses saved his people in battle by pleading to God with outstretched arms sustained by his captains; this child shall save with arms stretched out upon a cross, sustained by nails—rather, by love.

> (December 19) "O Root of Jesse, you stand for an ensign of mankind; before you kings shall keep silence, and to you all nations shall have recourse. Come, save us, and do not delay."[5]

David, son of Jesse, was a great king, but only a figure of the King who was to be the perfect flowering of that kingly line. A perfect flower has sprung up from poor humanity rooted in the dung heap of sin. Come! Do not delay!

> (December 20) "O Key of David and Scepter of the house of Israel: You open and no man closes; you close and no man opens. Come

> and deliver him from the chains of prison who sits in darkness and in the shadow of death."[6]

The ruling power shall be His. *The Lord God will give to him the throne of David his father.*[7] "Key of David"—He alone can make man free. He was sent to *proclaim liberty to captives....*[8]

> (December 21) "O Rising Dawn, Radiance of the Light eternal and Sun of Justice; come, and enlighten those who sit in darkness and in the shadow of death."[9]

The darkness of centuries begins to lift, the soft light of dawn breaks over Bethlehem's hills. Soon the full brightness of the eternal light, of the Sun of Justice, shall shine upon the whole world. So long, so very long, have men sat in darkness, in the shadow of death. Individually we must accept the light, for some show by evil deeds, toleration of injustice, that they prefer darkness.

> (December 22) "O King of the Gentiles and the desired of all, you are the cornerstone that binds two into one. Come, and save poor man whom you fashioned out of clay."[10]

Cornerstone uniting side and side, foundation and structure, in the temple of God; uniting Jew and pagan, the two great divisions in the mind of the Jewish theocracy. All who are to be part of the City of God are united and built upon Christ. *See, I am laying a cornerstone in Zion, an approved stone, and precious.*[11]

All are "fashioned out of clay," and no brick or tile is chosen because of its inherent worth. The choosing is a free gift of God, and we must give ourselves to the building up of His Church.

(December 23) "O Emmanuel, our King and Lawgiver, the Expected of nations and their Savior: come, and save us, O Lord our God!"[12]

What a meaningful list of names for us to dwell on: Emmanuel, King, Lawgiver, Savior, Lord, God.

"Emmanuel—God with us." What precious intimacies does this name recall, in the sacrifice and sacrament, in His Mystical Body, in the divine indwelling.

Come, Lord Jesus!

(The references for the antiphons themselves are generally not direct quotations but the source of inspiration for these prayers.)

1. Sir. 24:5; Wis. 8:1
2. Jn. 1:14
3. Jn. 1:3
4. Ex. 3:2, 20:1
5. Is. 11:10
6. Is. 22:22; Rv. 3:7; Lk. 1:79
7. Lk. 1:32-33
8. Lk. 4:18
9. Ps. 107:10
10. Hg. 2:8; Ep. 2:14, 20
11. 1 Pt. 2:6
12. Is. 7:14, 33:22

## The Advent

O come, Lord Jesus, Savior King,
and ransom to the captives bring;
from Satan's shackles free us.
You are the Light of life, the hope
of those who in sin's darkness grope—
O come, Lord Jesus!

O come as gently as the dew
and wearied, blighted hearts renew,
from passion's heat relieve us.
Like lightly, softly falling rain
that vivifies the earth in spring
come down, Lord Jesus!

Stir up Your might, O Lord, and come!
Your flock dispersed unite, make one;
O gentle Shepherd, lead us!
Make strife of troubled souls to cease,
reign now—and ever—Prince of Peace!
O come, Lord Jesus!

*You've come, O Jesus*—Light of Light
and God of God, and Lord of might—
but sweetly sense deceives us:
An infant, weak, dependent, mild,
a brother dear, a virgin's child,
You have come, Lord Jesus!

## Christmas Season

### A Christmas Prayer

The beams of His star light all your ways,
The peace song of angels fill all these days.
Bethlehem's tidings your spirit renew;
His pain and His want be comfort to you.
The smile of His Mother rest on your face.
The best of your gifts be His love and His grace.

## What a Blessed Pause Is Christmas

A brief respite from the restlessness and rush of our astronautical and computer-complex world...seeing in humble shepherds the contentment of simplicity.

A time of turning our ears from the din of confusing cries and conflicting claims that tear a troubled world, that divide a nation...to listen to—to dare trust—angels' promise of *peace*....

A moment of resting our eyes from the siege of endless images that allege the needs of the good life... to see that linen wraps and a hole in a hill are enough.

A time of revulsion at veneration of Venus, the cult of the body and disdain of the spirit...knowing that a Mary-like heart is the cradle of Christ.

A tranquil time when the Spirit of Love enlarges, ennobles our human loves....

The precious *Season of Grace,* when our prayer for each other is that *God's own peace, which is beyond all understanding, will keep our hearts and minds in Christ Jesus.*[1]

1. Cf. Phil. 4:7

## Merry Christmas!

Home in festive spirit,
tree-trimmed and holly-hung,
dens with hearth-fires, fragrant, friendly,
windows and doorways bright and expectant.

The Guest, He who brings life and light,
lies on the bedding of beasts
in a dark cave, cold, unclean.

## Happy Holiday!

Tables loaded, fruit of the fat fields,
gifts from the ends of the earth,
abundance beyond all needs.

He who feeds the flocks
draws life from lumps of decay-fed earth,
asks but the child's small needs,
the naked necessities.

## Joy to the Earth!

Merry music, television shows,
noise and nonsense filling minutes and minds
through all the day.

He is found in the peace of the deep night
under the silent stars,
where men may put the God-like powers
to contemplation of the Infinite.

Madonna!
Still you bring Him to us,
the gift of God, and your gift,
whenever we seek Him;
seek Him in the quiet corners of troubled hearts
in moments of wisdom,
setting aside the gilt trinkets,
conceding our poverty.
In sobering times of sorrow,
when peril impends,
Mother of Mercy, show us your Son!

## "Merry Christmas" and All That

So new each year, the story old,
as though it never had been told;
as fresh as night's untrodden snow,
as undimmed as the pole star's glow.

Now artists write or paint or sing
the glory of our Savior King;
and artless folk like you and me
pen heart-held greetings haltingly.

"A Merry Holiday," "Good Cheer,"
"The season's blessings through the year"—
a thousand phrasings have not brought
to rounded form the shapeless thought.

But come, let's drop the heavy pen,
make haste to our New Bethlehem,
and there at altar-crib we meet
to lay our thoughts at Jesus' feet.

And so we meet there Christmas Day
while time and distance fall away;
the living Christ receive, adore,
who makes us one forevermore.

Holy Family
(Sunday after Christmas)

Read Col. 3:12-21
Sir. 3:3-7, 14-17

# I Family—the Foundation

> *Have you not read that at the beginning the creator made them male and female and declared, 'For this reason a man shall leave his father and mother and cling to his wife, and the two shall become as one'? Thus they are no longer two but one flesh....*[1]

From "the beginning," then, before any history of civilization, the family was the basic unit of human living. A man and a woman, complementing each other physically and psychologically, needing each other; the child the fruit of their mutual love and self-giving, needing the warmth and stability of their love for his human development.

As a human institution, subject to exaggerated self-love, the family suffered many disorders and improprieties. In our times,

> "serious disturbances are caused in families by modern economic conditions, by influences at once social and psychological, and by the demands of civil society."[2]

However,

> "Christian spouses have a special sacrament by which they are fortified and receive a kind of consecration in the duties and dignities of their state."[3]

Can Nazareth's unique family, living in an era so vastly different from ours technologically, politically, sociologically, be a useful mirror for modern families? Paul's letter to his "family" at Colossae proposes virtues which are perennially necessary for the welfare of the family, as well as the larger society. It easily becomes a prayer for our families:

> O Father in heaven, You have chosen us to be holy; to be kind and humble, gentle and patient; to bear with one another's faults, forgiving each other as soon as a quarrel begins. We must forgive because You have forgiven us. Grant us an understanding of how much You *have* forgiven us. Put love into our hearts, which pulls together all these other things, sustains and perfects them. Let us appreciate that this love is not a soft, effusive, superficial feeling, but essentially something strong, motivating to constant consideration and kindness. Then will this basic love put Your Son's peace in our hearts, the peace of Nazareth in our homes.

## II Child Toward Parent

The first reading (Sir. 3:3-7, 14-17) provides a simple meditation on the how and why in honoring and loving parents.

The ideal is to grow and develop as Jesus did within His family. Except for the presentation at forty days and the incident in the temple at age twelve, we have only the lightest sketch of His life before His emergence into public activity. The few words are heavy with meaning. After His presentation in the temple, it is said, *The child grew in size and strength, filled with wisdom, and the grace of God was upon him.*[4] After the visit to the temple, we read, *He went down with them then, and came to Nazareth, and was obedient to them.... Jesus...progressed steadily in wisdom and age and grace before God and men.*[5] He accepted the authority of His parents; He grew in wisdom and in all moral and spiritual strengths, which gave Him favor with God and men. That is all—to cover thirty years. The Lord lived most of His life as an inconspicuous laboring man in an ordinary family. This major part of His life gives us the pattern that all of us may easily follow.

## III Parent Toward Child

Paul's last injunction in today's second reading is very important:

> *And fathers, do not nag your children lest they lose heart.*[6]

There is much in the world in which our young people are growing up that produces frustration and insecurity: war, need for greater education, job uncertainty, obvious flaws in "the system," the pressures of our value system to possess everything and enjoy every experience possible—to mention a few of the larger problems. Often their difficulties spring from objectively small, narrowly personal matters. They need above all to be *listened to*, respected—

never "written off" in anger. Great prudence and inexhaustible patience are required.

If as parents we have succeeded in giving our children a Christian sense of values, we can more confidently allow them a good measure of independence in young adulthood, even though this is a freedom also to make mistakes. They will have a basis for judging their mistakes and a power of recovery.

> Heavenly Father of all, give us mutual respect and trust, in love. "May the intercession of the virgin Mother of God and blessed Joseph ever bestow Your peace and grace upon our families, through Christ our Lord."[7]

1. Mt. 19:4-6
2. Vatican II, Church Today, 47, paragraph 2
3. Vatican II, Church Today, 48, paragraph 6
4. Lk. 2:40 (Gospel, B)
5. Lk. 2:51-52 (Gospel, C)
6. Col. 3:21
7. Prayer over the Gifts

Solemnity of Mary, Mother of God
(January 1)

Read Gal. 4:4-7

## I His Son, Born of a Woman

Man in moments of contemplation, searches for the meaning in all about him and of his own life. He searches ultimately, not always explicitly, for God, First Cause, Creator, End. Through the centuries, slowly and gradually, God reveals Himself—yet remains truly a hidden God. Finally He sends His Son, "born of a woman." He is one of us, with a human mind to communicate intimately on our own level; with a human heart to share our hopes and anxieties, our desires and repugnances, our sorrows and joys. He has blessed us with His sensible presence, He has "let his face shine upon us."

*This is how you shall bless the Israelites. Say to them:*
*The Lord bless you and keep you!*
*The Lord let his face shine on you and be gracious to you!*
*The Lord look upon you kindly and give you peace!*[1]

The role of the Virgin Mary is taken up by Vatican II as a section of the document on the Church. It begins with a quote from Galatians as found in today's second reading.

> "Wishing in his supreme goodness and wisdom to effect the redemption of the world, *when the fullness of time came, God sent his Son, born of a woman...that we might receive the adoption of sons* (Gal. 4:4-5). 'He for us men, and for our salvation, came down from heaven, and was incarnate by the Holy Spirit from the Virgin Mary' (Creed, Roman Mass)."[2]

> "...she is endowed with the supreme office and dignity of being the Mother of the Son of God. As a result she is also the favorite daughter of the Father and the temple of the Holy Spirit. Because of this gift of sublime grace she far surpasses all other creatures, both in heaven and on earth."[3]

## II We Also Are Sons

Jesus was born to enable us to be adopted as sons. In the Church we are one body with Christ, the head; we are sons of Mary.

> "...she is 'clearly the mother of the members of Christ...since she cooperated out of love so that there might be born in the Church the faithful, who are members of Christ their head.'"[4]

Having been born into the Church, having Mary as our mother, we have a special relationship with the three Persons of the Trinity, as she had.

Sons of the Father:

> *The proof that you are sons is the fact that God has sent forth into our hearts the spirit of his Son which cries out "Abba!" ("Father!")*[5]

Brothers of the Lord:

*Those whom he foreknew he predestined to share the image of his Son, that the Son might be the first-born of many brothers.*[6]

Bearers of the Spirit:

*...he will give you another Paraclete*
*to be with you always...*
*he remains with you*
*and will be within you.*[7]

Lord, let Your face shine on us!

1. Nm. 6:23-26 (first reading)
2. Vatican II, The Church, 52, paragraph 1
3. Vatican II, The Church, 53, paragraph 1
4. Vatican II, The Church, 53, paragraph 2
5. Gal. 4:6-7 (second reading)
6. Rom. 8:29
7. Jn. 14:16-17

When ancient Greek, with master sculptor's art
to stone his dream of Lady Love consigned,
such faultless form and line did he impart
that raptured eye regrets it's cold and blind.

Regrets 'tis only rude, insensate rock—
more perfect as it is than human mold—
ethereal maid that might earth's models mock;
unreal—unfleshed ideal that heavens hold.

That heaven held, indeed, but gave to earth
when Father planned the daughter of His pride;
when Word of God sought mother for His birth,
and Spirit formed and favored human bride.

Rejoice, O Maid most highly favored, blessed!
Far more than face and form would we extol.
But vain! There's no tongue-telling of the best:
the God-like glory of the full-graced soul.

Epiphany

Read Is. 60:1-6
Mt. 2:1-12

## I Rejoicing in Light

The whole of the Christmas cycle, including Advent's preparation and Epiphany's conclusion, is one long celebration of the Feast of Light. That short word for a wonderful physical reality is enriched by its application as a symbol of the Christian revelation and its radiance in our lives.

We celebrate the coming of the Redeemer with *the good news of peace....*[1] As we hear in the second reading,

> *It is no less than this: in Christ Jesus the Gentiles are now co-heirs with the Jews, members of the same body and sharers of the promise....*[2]

In the Gospel for the second Sunday after Christmas we listen to John's poetic introduction of the Word, the Light that has come into the world.

> *...the Word was God....*
> *Whatever came to be in him, found life,*
> *life for the light of men.*
> *The light shines on in darkness....*[3]

Today we shout with joy and urgency:

> *Rise up in splendor!*[4]

There came wise men who *observed his star at its rising.*[5] Since then all the wise men from the east and from the west, from the north and south, century after century, have searched for the source of the light that is in the world, the light that reveals the world's magnificence and meaning.

> *The real light which gives light to every man....*[6]
> *...the reflection of the Father's glory...he sustains all things by his powerful word.*[7]

Because of the many disorders in evidence all around us, we are inclined to agree that *darkness covers the earth, and thick clouds cover the peoples;* but our appreciation of the revelation we have received in the Church, and our trust in the Lord's fidelity and power, prompt us to cry out:

> *But upon you the Lord shines,*
> *and over you appears his glory.*

So we say, in fervent petition and indomitable optimism,

> *Nations shall walk by your light....*
> *Raise your eyes and look about;*
> *they all gather and come to you....*
> *Then you shall be radiant at what you see,*
> *your heart shall throb and overflow....*[8]

## II Giving Gifts

> *Then they opened their coffers and presented him with gifts of gold, frankincense, and myrrh.*[9]

Traditionally these gifts have definite significance: *gold,* wealth, for Jesus' kingship; *incense* for His divinity; *myrrh,* used in embalming, for His redeeming death.

As symbols of our own gifts to the Lord, gold may stand for our material resources; incense for our worship and praise; myrrh for our "little deaths," the suffering and self-denial involved in doing His will.

All gifts are symbolic, much more than a cheap or expensive *thing*. My gift says, here is something of *me:* what it cost me, my thought about you, my affection for you. A box of candy may say: your presence, your memory, is sweet to me. Cut flowers are significant because in giving a brief pleasure their very lives are sacrificed. A diamond is for entire self-commitment, with its sparkle of life and everlasting durability.

The culmination of giving is self-giving in reference to God, who has first given all we have and are. It may be a career dedication, turning all our resources of physical and mental energies to doing an excellent job that in some manner improves the city of man and so redounds to the glory of his Creator. It may be the dedication of marriage, a lifetime of self-discipline for the good and happiness of the marriage partner and the children. It could be the costly acceptance of Christ's invitation to a close imitation of Him in a religious consecration and apostolic life.

Like wise men, following a star, let us offer to others—ultimately to the Lord—our gifts of gold, frankincense and myrrh:

our disposition of things;
the fragrance of our prayers and love;
the myrrh of the little deaths to our ego;
readiness to be imposed upon, to defer to others.

1. Eph. 2:17
2. Eph. 3:6
3. Jn. 1:1, 4-5
4. Is. 60:1 (first reading)
5. Mt. 2:2
6. Jn. 1:9-10
7. Heb. 1:3
8. Cf. Is. 60:1-5 (first reading)
9. Mt. 2:11 (Gospel)

## Baptism of the Lord

Read Is. 42:1-4, 6-7
Mk. 1:6-11

### I Humble

Jesus begins His public life with an act of humility. Having come into this world, He was like us in everything, *yet never sinned.*[1] Now He voluntarily joins the ranks of sinners who come to John for baptism. Over John's protest, "*I should be baptized by you,*" He says simply, "*Give in for now. We must do this....*"[2]

Growth in spiritual life must be rooted in humility. It is an axiom that humility comes through actual humiliation. Jesus shows us the way here at the beginning of His public life, and the end of it will be in that apex of humiliation, His death on a cross.

It is interesting that the Father gives formal credentials to His Son while Jesus stands among sinners as though one of them, just out of the water, His outer robe flung over His soaked undergarments, hair disheveled and dripping. God again ratifies the dignity of the Messiah-King, with upheavals in nature and the dead rising, while that King hangs naked on the cross. (In rating a man's worth, do I place too great a weight, perhaps instinctively, on externals: grooming, urbanity, circumspect speech and approved behavior?)

Alcoholics Anonymous, which has been so powerful a help to moral and spiritual recovery for alcoholics, wisely makes humility the basic first steps: "We admitted we were powerless...that our lives had become unmanageable...admitted to God, ourselves, and another human being the exact nature of our wrongs."[3]

## II Gentle and Strong

These two characteristics of the Lord in His ministry are described in the first reading:

> *...Not crying out, not shouting,*
> *not making his voice heard in the street.*
> *A bruised reed he shall not break,*
> *and a smoldering wick he shall not quench,*
> *until he establishes justice upon the earth....*[4]

We have seen His gentleness in dealing with little children, with lepers, the blind and lame, fallen women and other sinners. We have seen Him strong in His confrontation with those who profaned His Father's house with their business; aggressive and fearless in denouncing hypocrites, the phony among rulers and religious leaders. The only sinners who received harsh treatment from Jesus were those who did not admit sin.

## III Favored Son

In the Gospels for all cycles the three synoptics give very similar accounts. We have a voice from heaven giving the credentials of Jesus: *"You are my beloved Son. On you my favor rests."*[5] He is filled with the Holy Spirit. He will give this Spirit to those who follow Him and work with Him: *He will baptize you in the Holy Spirit and in fire.*[6] We see that as the Father gives the Spirit to the Son, the Son also gives the Spirit to us.

Peter says of Jesus that God had

> *...anointed him with the Holy Spirit and power. He went about doing good works and healing all who were in the grip of the devil....*[7]

Jesus is ready to give us some of His own power, to baptize us with the Holy Spirit and fire so that we too may go about doing good and helping to save those who have fallen into the power of evil.

> Father, thank You for sending us the Son in whom You are delighted, endowing Him with Your Spirit, giving Him power to free us from captivity and darkness. May He renew in us that baptism of the Holy Spirit by which we also are made pleasing to You.

1. Heb. 4:15
2. Mt. 3:14-15 (Gospel, A)
3. 12 Steps AA
4. Is. 42:2-4
5. Lk. 3:22
6. Lk. 3:16
7. Acts 10:38 (second reading)

First Sunday of Lent

Read Gn. 2:7-9, 3:1-7
(A, B)

# I Freedom and Temptation

Man is by nature free; that freedom is of first importance to men today, and there is general concern about any condition that makes man less free, be it social, economic, political, psychological. Freedom is equally subject to use and misuse. With the first misuse of freedom by Eve and Adam, man was deeply hurt in his capacity to exercise both freedom and intelligence.

In the documents of Vatican II we read:

> ...authentic freedom is an exceptional sign of the divine image within man. For God has willed that man be left "in the hand of his own counsel" so that he can seek his Creator spontaneously, and come freely to utter blissful perfection through loyalty to Him. Hence man's dignity demands that he act according to a knowing and free choice.[1]

> ...from the very dawn of history man abused his liberty.... What divine revelation makes known to us agrees with experience. Examining his heart, man finds that he has inclina-

> tions toward evil too, and is engulfed by manifold ills which cannot come from his good Creator.... Therefore man is split within himself....[2]

There is evident contrast in the behavior under temptation of our mother Eve and of Christ who gives us spiritual life: Eve tunes in to temptation, listens willingly to the voice of evil. *The woman saw that the tree was good for food, pleasing to the eyes, and desirable for gaining wisdom.* Jesus turns it off immediately, thinking of His Father and not of His own needs. *Man does not live by bread alone....*

Eve weighs God's word and a contrary word: *You shall not eat it or even touch it, lest you die,* against *You certainly will not die.* Jesus counters every word of the tempter with the word of God. No contrary word has any weight whatever. Eve is open to possibilities other than those God has indicated: *...you will be like gods*—so why be dependent? *...who know what is good and what is bad*—decide for yourself what is good for you and what is evil. But Jesus says man directs his life by *every utterance that comes from the mouth of God.*[3]

## II Sense of Sin

> *She also gave some to her husband...and he ate it. Then the eyes of both of them were opened and they realized that they were naked.*[4]

They saw clearly now, but it was evil they saw, within themselves, and shame was born. *...know what is good and what is bad:* they know evil now in the biblical sense of experiencing. There was only pain in this knowledge.

We are to enter into the paschal mystery through a deep sense of sin and an acute awareness of our need of Christ's redeeming act.

> O God, grant us this sense of sin. Help us to take on the psalmist's sorrowing spirit as we pray his repentant words:
>
> *Have mercy on me, O God, in your goodness;*
> *in the greatness of your compassion wipe out my offense.*
> *Thoroughly wash me from my guilt*
> *and of my sin cleanse me.*
>
> *For I acknowledge my offense,*
> *and my sin is before me always:*
> *"Against you only have I sinned,*
> *and done what is evil in your sight...."*[5]

## III Joyful Hope

A joyful and grateful confidence in Christ must counterbalance a sense of our sinfulness. Paul happily compares the fall in Adam and the restoration in Christ.

> *In the first case sentence followed upon one offense and brought condemnation, but in the second, the gift came after many offenses and brought acquittal...those who receive the overflowing grace and gift of justice live and reign through the one man, Jesus Christ.*[6]
>
> *Remember that your compassion, O Lord,*
> *and your kindness are from of old.*
> *The sins of my youth and my frailties remember not;*

*in your kindness remember me*
*because of your goodness, O Lord.*
*Good and upright is the Lord;*
*thus he shows sinners the way.*
*He guides the humble to justice,*
*he teaches the humble his way.*[7]

1. Church Today, 17, paragraph 2
2. Church Today, 13, paragraph 1, 2, 3
3. Cf. Gn. 2:7-9; 3:1-7 and Mt. 4:1-11 (first reading and Gospel, A)
4. Gn. 3:6-7
5. Ps. 51:3-6 (responsorial psalm, A)
6. Rom. 5:16-17 (second reading, A)
7. Ps. 25:6-9 (responsorial psalm, B)

## Second Sunday of Lent

Read Mt. 17:1-9
Gn. 22:1-2, 9-18
(A, C, B)

### I Glory and Humiliation

On this early Sunday in Lent, the season in which we recall the sufferings of Christ and our sinfulness, the Gospel strangely presents to us a glorified Christ. The cross and the resurrection are inseparable. The Lord's suffering, death, and glorification are one redeeming mystery. The witnesses of His transfiguration, Peter, James and John, are the same three who will be close to Him in Gethsemani to witness His humiliation.

Peter, enraptured by the glory of Jesus, says, "*Master, how good it is for us to be here.*" He wants to remain, but significantly, *He did not really know what he was saying.*[1] This glorification of His Master was a passing moment. The vision dissolved, and *they did not see anyone but Jesus.*[2] This is our usual way of companionship with Jesus, an ordinary Jesus, neither glorified nor greatly suffering but a man going about doing good. We have our occasional exultations, our joys and our sufferings. As with Jesus, our Easter joy is full and permanent only after death. There should be an integrating, peaceful acceptance of joy and sorrow, pain and well-being, as the way of redemption in Christ.

## II Enemies of the Cross

There are Christians who do not live by faith, accepting their share in the cross:

> *Unfortunately, many go about in a way that shows them to be enemies of the cross of Christ...I say it with tears. Such as these will end in disaster! Their god is their belly and their glory is in their shame. I am talking about those who are set upon the things of this world.*[3]

Are "the things of this world" unimportant then? They are, of course, important and good, but only proportionately, when and in the measure that they serve our ultimate human dignity and destiny. *We have our citizenship in heaven.* For some of Paul's Philippians, food and pleasures had evidently become too important. Our bodies are a remarkable creation but not the noblest part of us. And there are times, as in sickness and old age, when we readily agree with Paul's description, *this lowly body of ours.* The transfiguration and the resurrection, mark

> *...our savior, the Lord Jesus Christ. He will give a new form to this lowly body of ours and remake it according to the pattern of his glorified body....*[4]

> *I believe that I shall see the bounty of the Lord*
> *in the land of the living.*
> *Wait for the Lord with courage;*
> *be stouthearted, and wait for the Lord.*[5]

# III Redemption Through Faith

The first readings for this Sunday, all three cycles, are about Abraham, "our father in faith." Like him, we are to believe even when circumstances make faith seem unreasonable. He was ready to sacrifice his son, though God had promised previously that through this son he would have descendants as numerous as the sands on the seashore.

God spared Abraham's son; He would have gained nothing from the sacrifice. But His own Son He did not spare, because His death was required for our salvation. God

> *...did not spare his own Son but handed him over for the sake of us all....*[6]

Our Faith holds to this wondrous love of God, that He gave up His Son to death, and so doing, *has robbed death of its power and has brought life and immortality into clear light through the gospel.*[7]

> *Our soul waits for the Lord,*
> *who is our help and our shield....*
> *May your kindness, O Lord, be upon us*
> *who have put our hope in you.*[8]

1. Lk. 9:33 (Gospel, C)
2. Mt. 17:8 (Gospel, A)
3. Phil. 3:18-19 (second reading, C) (The majority of commentators think that Paul here refers to Judaizers who emphasized circumcision, dietary observance, etc., rather than the death-resurrection event that effects salvation. However, some commentators believe he refers to libertine Christians.)
4. Phil. 3:20-21
5. Ps. 27:13-14 (responsorial psalm, C)
6. Rom. 8:32 (second reading, B)
7. 2 Tm. 1:10 (second reading, A)
8. Ps. 33:20, 22 (responsorial psalm, A)

## Surrender

The cross, O Lord, Your cross!
  Of self-willed ease enough!
The polished joys prove gloss;
  I'll take the timbers rough.

Though I walked sweet paths of May
  The cross moved with me yet;
Dark shadow through the day,
  At night, dim silhouette.

Each sainted friend in heaven
  Of whom I asked the good
One selfsame word has given:
  "Take up the blood-stained wood."

O Love's most certain token!
  Too long despised, ill used—
Lord, lest this reed be broken,
  Grant strength to be infused.

## Third Sunday of Lent

Read Jn. 4:5-26, 39-42
Ps. 19:7-10
(A, B)

### I Springs of Water

Unless experienced, it is probably impossible to know fully the agony of great thirst, the exhaustion, the pain of the whole physical being crying out for this element most essential to its functions and life. To the people of Palestine, living on the fringe of desert area, the figure of "living water," of flowing streams, of clear, cold water from wells and springs, was most meaningful. In the dry lands a source of water is the difference between dead land and living fertile soil. Water means life. The image runs through the Old Testament, and Jesus appropriated it to convey His own message, the good news of eternal life.

*If only you recognized God's gift,*
*and who it is that is asking you for a drink,*
*you would have asked him instead,*
*and he would have given you living water.*[1]

During Lent we ask more earnestly for the living water. Our soul is a desert, all the seeds of our talents and potential lying dormant. From the deep springs of Christ's divinity flow the waters that waken to growth and fruitfulness.

> *...give me this water, sir, so that I shall not grow thirsty....*[2]

The life-giving water is free to all who really desire it:

> *Let him who is thirsty come forward; let all who desire it accept the gift of life-giving water.*[3]

## II Broken Cisterns

We may neglect these waters of life and drink from other sources. But we are not completely satisfied, are left still thirsting; or the sources dry up.

> *They have forsaken me, the source of living waters;*
> *They have dug themselves cisterns,*
> *broken cisterns, that hold no water.*[4]

In our less-than-Utopian world, with its divisions and tensions, where no man is completely happy and without further desires, definite or vague, humanity proclaims its mighty thirst for the living God.

> *O God, you are my God whom I seek;*
> *for you my flesh pines and my soul thirsts*
> *like the earth, parched, lifeless and without water.*[5]

Some men today, intent on personal freedom, rebel at the very form of the Lord's Commandments: "Thou shalt not...." They would have no one, even God, tell them that certain actions are forbidden them. Although such an attitude of man before his Creator cannot be justified, it does seem so much easier to accept God's word when we see it as directing us, with love, to positive actions required by our nature for fulfillment and joy, giving our lives integrity and peace. In the responsorial psalm for cycle B, the Law of the Lord is spoken of in this attractive, positive aspect: it is "sweet as honey," "giving wisdom," "rejoicing the heart," "enlightening the eye." He who sees the Law of the Lord in this way has found a fountain of pure water. He who looks upon it as a set of restraining rules will dig his own leaking cistern.

On a festival in Jerusalem Jesus had cried out His invitation for all who were thirsty to come to Him and drink. The proffered "fountains of living water" were the Spirit to be given in Baptism to believers. With the Spirit we have a saturation of blessings, for He "pours" the love of God into our hearts.[6]

*As the hind longs for the running waters,*
*so my soul longs for you, O God.*
*Athirst is my soul for God, the living God.*[7]

1. Jn. 4:10 (Gospel, A)
2. Jn. 4:15
3. Rv. 22:17
4. Jer. 2:13
5. Ps. 63:2
6. Cf. Rom. 5:5
7. Ps. 42:2-3

## Fourth Sunday of Lent

Read Lk. 15:1-3, 11-32
(C)

It is presumptuous to add to that perfect story, that exquisite gem, in the fifteenth chapter of Luke (Gospel for cycle C) called variously "The Prodigal Son," "The Lost Son and the Dutiful Son," or perhaps more properly, "The Forgiving Father." The packed sentences should be slowly pondered, keeping in mind that it is the picture given us by Jesus of His Father's mercy, pausing at any response of mind or heart to this Father's remarkable love *for us*.

Presumptuously, there follow a few observations, which should be referred to only if curiosity should lead one, after meditating, to compare thoughts.

> The younger son asks for his inheritance: not something really due him but the gift of his father. He squanders it—as we waste gifts, graces, opportunities.
>
> What a picture of the wretchedness of one who has left his Father through sin: lonely, hungry, ragged and dirty; humiliated in feeding pigs; remorseful and hopeless.
>
> The great decision: *I will break away and return to my father, and say to him, "Father... I no longer deserve to be called your son. Treat me like one of your hired hands."* He might have resolved to say, "Sir,..."—but it is still

"Father." That relationship never changes for us, either, no matter what malice or wretchedness we fall into.

*While he was still a long way off....* God is waiting for our return, always, respecting our freedom, which is essentially what makes us His image and makes *love* possible. *His mercy endures forever,*[1] but He must wait for us freely to return.

*Let us eat and celebrate:* suggests the intimate connection of repentance and eucharist, of reconciliation and celebration—perhaps better expressed in a present-day practice of having a common penance service preceding the liturgical celebration.

We may be a little inclined to sympathize with the older, faithful son, but still, *everything I have is yours.* He fails, as we often do, in imitating his father's mercy. We see by his words that he is not ready to enter into this celebration of family love: *this son of yours*—not "my brother."

We, like the older son, sometimes show ourselves unlike our Father in His desire for easy reconciliation. In the second reading (C) Paul says he is given the work of reconciliation, and is thus an ambassador of Christ. He is an apostle, of course, but all of us should have at heart the work of trying to help men to understand and imitate the merciful love of God. Jesus' blessing on peacemakers is for every Christian.

In this parable Jesus shows us the mercy of His Father. The Son's merciful love is exactly like the Father's, and this easy reconciliation is possible for us only because of the Son's self-sacrifice. *For our sakes God made him who did not know sin to be sin, so that in him we might become the very holiness of God.*[2]

*I will bless the Lord at all times,*
*his praise shall be ever in my mouth.*
*Let my soul glory in the Lord;*
*the lowly will hear me and be glad.*

*Look to him that you may be radiant with joy,*
*and your faces may not blush with shame.*[3]

1. Ps. 118
2. 2 Cor. 5:21
3. Ps. 34:2-3, 6 (responsorial psalm, C)

Fifth Sunday of Lent

Read Jn. 11:1-45
(A)

# I Graves, Tombs and Tears

The various readings for this Sunday present images of graves and tombs, weeping and death.

> *Then you shall know that I am the Lord, when I open your graves and have you rise from them, O my people.*[1]

Is there a more poignant memory than that of standing by an open grave, looking upon the box that holds the remains of a loved one about to be disposed of, put under the earth and out of the vibrant, living world forever? We are not surprised to find Jesus sharing this universal human pain.

> *Jesus began to weep.*[2]

What a burden of meaning is carried in these few words. In all of Scripture are there words more revealing of the heart of Christ, more consoling to suffering man? The human tears of God-made-man have mingled with that flow which began with the tears of Eve weeping over her son murdered by his brother, and with the centuries has become an increasing flood gathering together the tributaries of pain that cover the earth.

Even Christ cannot dry up this flood; sin and suffering remain as man's constant companions. And always there is death, unfailing source of tears. But He, the resurrection and the life, has distilled from our tears the bitter salt of despair, and through them we are able to catch the glimmer of a new life which He has won by bearing our sorrows. Because of the Lord's sympathetic loving even to death, we are heirs to a perfect life in a renewed creation, where God *shall wipe every tear from their eyes, and there shall be no more death or mourning, crying out or pain....*[3]

## II Beautiful Cemeteries

Perhaps you have visited a cemetery on some serene summer day and found it a place of beauty and peace. Sunshine filtering through the trees, the shadows dancing on a smooth lawn, varied shades of green shrubbery and bright flowers, a few bird songs —all these inducing a tranquillity of spirit. The living landscape speaks reassuringly to us, even while we know of disintegration beneath the earth. There is significance in the polished beauty of the granite stone, unweathered, unchanged over decades, even centuries. And while it stands over decay and dissolution, it bears a name, sharp and ineffaceable, witnessing to an immortal personality. Beneath that name might be engraved the psalmist's words:

*I trust in the Lord;*
*my soul trusts in his word.*
*My soul waits for the Lord....*[4]

On a day to come, a voice of command will call forth this spirit in its restored body, even as happened at Bethany:

*Lazarus, come out!*

for

*I am the resurrection and the life:*
*whoever believes in me,*
*though he should die, will come to life....*[5]

Only sin is in opposition to life and resurrection. The responsorial psalms for Cycles A and B invite us to enter the final weeks of Lent with a more intense sense of sinfulness, but with confidence of mercy.

*If you, O Lord, mark iniquities,*
*Lord, who can stand?*
*But with you is forgiveness,*
*that you may be revered.*[6]

*Have mercy on me, O God, in your goodness;*
*in the greatness of your compassion wipe out my offense.*
*Thoroughly wash me from my guilt....*[7]

The psalm for Cycle C gives a balance of joy to the two penitential psalms above, joy in the return of those who were chained by death and by sin: *everyone who lives in sin is the slave of sin.*[8]

*When the Lord brought back the captives of Zion,*
*we were like men dreaming.*
*Then our mouth was filled with laughter,*
*and our tongue with rejoicing.*

*Those that sow in tears*
*shall reap rejoicing.*

*Although they go forth weeping,*
*carrying the seed to be sown,*
*They shall come back rejoicing,*
*carrying their sheaves.*[9]

*The Lord has done great things for us;*
*we are filled with joy.*[10]

1. Ez. 37:13 (first reading, A)
2. Jn. 11:35 (Gospel, A)
3. Rv. 21:4
4. Ps. 130:5-6 (responsorial psalm, A)
5. Jn. 11:25 (Gospel, A)
6. Ps. 130:3-4 (responsorial psalm, A)
7. Ps. 51:3-4 (responsorial psalm, B)
8. Jn. 8:34
9. Ps. 126:1-2, 5-6
10. Responsorial antiphon, C

# I Who Struck You?

*Then they began to spit in his face and hit him. Others slapped him, saying: 'Play the prophet for us, Messiah! Who struck you?'*[1]

It was Pilate's soldiers who struck you, Jesus. What have I to do with this pitiless mockery and brutality? I believe You to be Lord, the Son of God and my Savior, and I honor and reverence You.

Do I really dare to repeat that question put to You so long ago, "Who hit you?" If I do, You will reply, with hurt but not with anger, "*You* hit me." And if I see as comforting insulation the centuries that stand between the actions before Pilate and the high priest and my own actions today, it is I who am blindfolded, Lord, not You. Though You seemed blindfolded, You saw perfectly the personal actions and intentions of those guards, and You see my own today. In Your divine presence the veil of time and distance melt away like the white snow-cover before a bright spring sun, exposing the dark earth of my soul.

Yes, I struck You when I sinned; each time I showed contempt for Your words, Your directives. Although You are now glorified and untouched personally by my evil actions, in some mysterious manner I still hit You when I strike some other man—hurt You by hurting him, by any kind of injustice, any selfish and thoughtless action, any refusal to love. *...as often as you did it for one of my least brothers, you did it for me.*[2]

I was very foolish, Lord, to think a blindfold could keep Your eyes from searching out my own as You respond to my question, "Who hit you, Christ?"

## II Why Hit Me?

> *Pilate's next move was to take Jesus and have him scourged. The soldiers then wove a crown of thorns and fixed it on his head.... Repeatedly they came up to him and said, "All hail, King of the Jews!" slapping his face as they did so.*[3]

A deep, instinctive resentment wells up in us at being slapped in the face. It is borne with greater difficulty than more damaging blows to the body, for it seems to touch more directly our essential human dignity, to reach the depths of our being. The natural response is swift retaliation. Jesus does not retaliate; He meekly suffers it—He who bears the dignity of the divine nature.

> *...one of the guards who was standing nearby gave Jesus a sharp blow on the face. "Is that the way to answer the high priest?" he said. Jesus replied, "If I said anything wrong produce the evidence, but if I spoke the truth why hit me?"*[4]

Lord Jesus, I find no real answer to this *why* when You put it to *me.* The perverseness of my heart sometimes amazes even myself. I have failed to live in Your presence. I have not looked directly and understandingly at Your face, bruised, bleeding, smeared with spittle. I have avoided those piercing, reproachful eyes. Yes, I have mocked and struck You. I am sorry.

1. Mt. 26:67-68 (Gospel, A) 2. Mt. 25:40 3. Jn. 19:1-3 4. Jn. 18:22-23

## I He Suffers Freely

The passion of Christ is fitting subject matter for prayer at any time in Lent but especially proper in the last week. The sufferings and death of the Lord lend themselves to prayer of affections, the heart often responding easily without labor of mind. Any part of the passion is matter for contemplation, a looking with faith and compassion on the suffering Christ.

St. Ignatius[1] gives us important guidelines to elicit a proper response:

Notice that the divinity is hidden now, and Jesus truly suffers as man, in body and mind.

*Though he was in the form of God,*
*he did not deem equality with God*
*something to be grasped at.*
*Rather, he emptied himself*
*and took the form of a slave,*
*being born in the likeness of men.*[2]

He could have destroyed and humiliated His enemies, but He is entirely passive in pain and humiliation.

Jesus suffers *freely*, He embraces the suffering, because of His love and my need:

*I have a baptism to receive. What anguish I feel till it is over!*[3]

*...on coming into the world, Jesus said:*
*"Sacrifice and offering you did not desire,*
*but a body you have prepared for me....*
*Then I said,...*
*'I have come to do your will, O God.'"*[4]

*The Father loves me for this:*
*that I lay down my life....*
*No one takes it from me;*
*I lay it down freely.*[5]

## II For Me

It is most important to realize my own involvement. This action I watch is not an incident in Roman or Jewish history, or a play that engages my emotions for an hour. Christ is living; the mysteries of His life are still lived out in my today. An all-pervasive divine love is embracing me now, and reaching out to others through me. And it may be that the Redeemer is using some pain, anxiety or sorrow of mine towards the redemption of others. As long as men inhabit the earth, He remains in it to save and give eternal life:

*Jesus Christ is the same yesterday, today, and forever.*[6]

It was given to the writer in Isaiah to express in vivid terms the intimate personal relationship of Jesus, this "suffering servant of the Lord," with his contemporaries some five hundred years before Christ's appearance—and with me, today, two thousand years after:

*...a man of suffering...*
*spurned, and we held him in no esteem.*

*Yet it was* our *infirmities that he bore,*
our *sorrows that he endured....*
*But he was pierced for* our *offenses,*
*crushed for our sins;*
*Upon him was the chastisement that makes us whole,*
*by his stripes we are healed.*
*...the Lord laid upon him*
*the guilt of us all.*[7]

1. Cf. Spiritual Exercises, numbers 195-197
2. Phil. 2:6-7
3. Lk. 12:50
4. Heb. 10:5-7
5. Jn. 10:17-18
6. Heb. 13:8
7. Cf. Is. 53:3, 4, 5

## Holy Thursday

Read Ex. 12:1-8, 11-14
Jn. 13:1-15

## I Remembrance

In the first reading we have a description of the Jewish Passover which the Lord was celebrating on the evening before His death, and which He was fulfilling. God used Moses to deliver the Hebrews from slavery, a "passover" to a new, free life. They were saved from the death visited upon the Egyptians by the sign of sacrificial blood sprinkled on their doorposts:

> *Seeing the blood, I will pass over you; thus, when I strike the land of Egypt, no destructive blow will come upon you.*[1]

In the second reading Jesus is seen as offering His own blood, to be shed on the following day, as the pledge of our freedom and life. Through all the centuries we, His followers, are to celebrate this new passover. We possess the freedom of God's children and the very life of God by a union with Jesus Christ, through the partaking of His body and blood.

> *For my flesh is real food*
> *and my blood real drink....*
> *Just as the Father who has life sent me*

*and I have life because of the Father,*
*so the man who feeds on me*
*will have life because of me.*[2]

We commemorate the *death* of the Lord but even more the love that He was showing us; so it is a feast, a celebration, as was the first passover:

*This day shall be a memorial feast for you,*
*which all your generations shall celebrate....*[3]

*How shall I make a return to the Lord*
*for all the good he has done for me?*
*The cup of salvation I will take up,*
*and I will call upon the name of the Lord....*

*To you will I offer sacrifice of thanksgiving...*
*in the presence of all his people.*[4]

## II Presence

Holy Thursday is traditionally a time when we specially honor Jesus in the Blessed Sacrament. Happy are we if we are drawn by this presence of Christ, drawn to easy converse with Him. In the power of His divinity He is present everywhere, but the thought of God as "pure spirit" is something of an obstacle to human communication. Is not this presence under the simple sign of bread akin to the presence experienced by John and Andrew early in the public life when Jesus invited them to come to where He was staying and they *stayed with him that day?*[5] Or to His presence to the two disciples when He was walking to Emmaus with them, revealing God's plan and finally Himself by "breaking bread" for them? And to Mary Magdalene when at the tomb she suddenly knew Him by His familiar address, "Mary," which caused her to cling to His feet in a surge of Easter joy?

> Jesus, make our hearts burn within us as You reveal Yourself in that intimate, blessed presence in the bread You break for us.

In the Old Testament God made His presence specially felt in the Ark of the Covenant and then in the temple at Jerusalem; in the New, upon our altars. We seem to need a locus of the human-divine presence, though the power and effect of that presence follow us everywhere, penetrating our being always. We should be drawn to that locus, fascinated by the nucleus of that bright flame which is God's love for us in the heart of Christ.

## III Example

The continued sacramental presence of Jesus is a striking manifestation of His love. Is the perfect return of that love best expressed in long prayers before the tabernacle? In great warmth of feeling and lyric praise? In doing great things for him? These are certainly good, but not always possible. It seems that a fitting response of love is not so difficult as to be out of reach for any of us. In the Gospel John writes:

> *He had loved his own in this world, and would show his love for them to the end.*[6]

And what follows? Jesus washes the feet of His disciples: humble service is love in action.

> *Such as my love has been for you,*
> *so must your love be for each other.*[7]

We are slow to accept this as the way to observe the "new commandment." It would make servants of the most dignified leaders, whether in the Church or in society.

> *"Do you understand what I just did for you?*
> *You address me as 'Teacher' and 'Lord,'*
> *and fittingly enough,*
> *for that is what I am.*
> *But if I washed your feet...*
> *then you must wash each other's feet."*[8]

> Lord, there are many ways of "washing each other's feet." Make me understand this, to see the opportunities, to gladly give simple, humble service to others.

1. Ex. 12:13
2. Jn. 6:55, 57
3. Ex. 12:14
4. Ps. 116:12-13, 17, 18 (responsorial psalm)
5. Jn. 1:39
6. Jn. 13:1
7. Jn. 13:34
8. Jn. 13:12-14

Good Friday

# The Suffering Christ

From the Old Testament

*...they who see me*
*abroad flee from me.*
*I am forgotten like the*
*unremembered*
*dead.*[1]

From the Gospels

*Jesus knew from the start, of course, the ones who refused to believe.... Many of his disciples broke away and would not remain in his company any longer.*[2]

Lord, You are saddened by some of us as we leave You, stop going with You, when we cease to join You regularly in Your offering of Yourself to the Father in the liturgical memorial of Your death and celebration of Your love. Perhaps we have left You by ignoring the teaching of Your Church—though You said to Your apostles, "Anyone who listens to you listens to me; anyone who rejects you rejects me...." We may be refusing the eucharistic Bread of Life whose giving cost You Your death; or neglecting the sacrament of forgiveness which was Your Easter gift, for our peace. Lord, to whatever degree we have left You, bring us back again to following You in faith and love.

*He was spurned and avoided by men....*[3]

*...the scribes and high priests tried to get their hands on him....*[4]

*...he surrendered himself to death*
*and was counted among the wicked;*
*And he shall take away the sins of many*
*and win pardon for their offenses.*[5]

*...I lay down my life.*
*...No one takes it from me;*
*I lay it down freely.*[6]

Jesus, give us a firm conviction that Your love brought You to freely taking upon Yourself our sins and the penalties they deserve. Even in extreme agony You were praying for us: "Father, forgive them; they don't know what they are doing." We who have been taught about sin and redemption, and have believed, ought much better to know what we are doing. But let Your prayer stand for us too, for who can fully understand sin: its power to destroy man and to reject divine love.

*But I am a worm, not a man;*
*the scorn of men, despised by the people....*[7]

*People going by kept insulting him.... The chief priests, the scribes, and the elders also joined in the jeering....*[8]

Lord Jesus, when we see You so humiliated, how can we be so sensitive about respect due us, so touchy about the least criticism? Are You to bear all the dishonor of our sinfulness and we none of it?

*...like a shoot from the parched earth....*[9]

*My throat is dried up*
*like baked clay,*
*my tongue cleaves to*
*my jaws....*[10]

*"I am thirsty."*[11]

We have been told of the tormenting thirst of crucifixion. Lord, let us realize also that greater thirst in the depths of Your being, for our good and a return of Your own love. In Your desires and self-offering, You were "like water draining away," emptied, receiving no compensating return.

*...they shall look on him whom they have thrust through, and they shall mourn for him as one mourns for an only son....*[12]

*One of the soldiers thrust a lance into his side....*[13]

*With age-old love I have*
*loved you;*
*so I have kept my*
*mercy toward you.*[14]

*There is no greater love*
*than this:*
*to lay down one's life*
*for one's friends.*
*You are my friends....*[15]

Thank You, Jesus, for calling us friends, for loving us with an everlasting love; for being so constant in Your love when we are so undependable.

1. Ps. 31:12-13 (responsorial psalm)
2. Jn. 6:64, 66
3. Is. 53:3 (first reading)
4. Lk. 20:19
5. Is. 53:12
6. Jn. 10:17-18
7. Ps. 22:7
8. Mt. 27:39, 41
9. Is. 53:2 (first reading)
10. Ps. 22:15
11. Jn. 19:28 (Gospel)
12. Zec. 12:10
13. Jn. 19:34
14. Jer. 31:3
15. Jn. 15:13-14

"All you that pass, attend and see
 if there be sorrow like to mine!"
So echoes from dark Calvary's tree
 a cry of grief and love divine.

"O my people, answer true,
 what evil is it I have done?
In what have I offended you?
 Give answer now!" But there is none.

For some may see and stay to mock;
 and others idly pause to stare.
But most pass by—no time to stop,
 for hearts are dull and do not care.

The ages through this heart has yearned,
 and will forever make complaint;
for though eternal love be spurned
 eternal patience cannot faint.

# Easter Vigil

*Simeon...said to Mary..."This child is destined to be a sign that will be opposed—and you yourself shall be pierced with a sword....*[1]

*Near the cross of Jesus there stood his mother.... When Jesus took the wine, he said, "Now it is finished." Then he bowed his head and delivered over his spirit.... They took Jesus' body and...bound it up in wrappings of cloth....*[2]

We contemplate you, sorrowing Mother, as you sit holding the limp body of your Son on your knees, in the manner of Michelangelo's Pietá. A little gesture of your left hand says, "Come and see. This is the rejected One, my Son. This is what is left to me, this marked and mangled thing. Come and see."

I kneel beside you, trying to understand the mystery of Christ. Trying to understand the fierce malice of sin. Trying to realize a measure and manner of love that allows the destruction of self.

Strangely still now, the feet which were once so restless, covered with the dust of all the roads men move on, marked by the stones of the rough ways in which the poor of the world walk.

So quiet now, those hands that ceaselessly blessed, touched the heads of children and the sores of lepers, beckoned the detested tax gatherer and raised up the fallen woman to human dignity.

So still the fingers that pointed up unpalatable parables and pointed out unjust officials and dishonest priests. The gashed hands paid dearly for these activities. We tried to keep them still with nails.

The lacerated back—so many welts and cuts—was all this done by a Roman soldier? But we know it was not. Many of us joined in this terrible game of afflicting the body of Christ.

Those purpled shoulders, they bore the burdens of all the over-burdened of the world. *We* could have lightened the load. Though we had little baggage ourselves, we sometimes ignored the huge bundle another was struggling with. We were pressed for time, occupied with important business, and so we avoided the eyes that searched for help. And now we recall the words,...*as often as you neglected to do it to one of these least ones, you neglected to do it to me.*[3]

Holy Mother, pierce me through!
In my heart each wound renew
of my Savior crucified.

Let me share with you His pain
who for all our sins was slain,
who for me in torments died.[4]

Yes, *for me* He died. This I wish ever to believe more firmly, understand more deeply. Mother most merciful, you forgive us as your Son Himself forgives. You and He only ask that we begin anew—ever beginning—to love.

O sweet Mother! Fount of love,
touch my spirit from above;
make my heart with yours accord.

Make me feel as you have felt;
make my soul to glow and melt
with the love of Christ my Lord.[5]

1. Lk. 2:34-35
2. Jn. 19:25, 30, 40
3. Mt. 25:45
4. Sequence, our Lady of Sorrows, "Stabat Mater"
5. *Ibid.*

## Easter Sunday

Read Jn. 20:1-18

"I arose and am still with you."[1]

Be glad, my heart!
Every heart!
The Sun has risen upon a world reborn.
This is an everlasting morning,
  dew-washed, pine-fresh, flower-fragrant.
A new, free morning—
  no clinging phantasms of a feverish night.
Clear, cool,
  glistening in hope, dripping with joy.
A morning for song,
  a hundred harmonies on one full, flowing word:
Alleluia!
Morning for the love song.
He who loved too much
  has gone through a cruel night of pain and rejection.
He has returned!
He is with us!
More humanly loving than ever,
In faith's vision, majestic, glorious,
  our God.

*Rabboni!*

*My Lord and my God!*

Love's way is to share: to share in pain and sorrow and difficulty; to share in joy, well-being, prosperity. We pray to share in the joy of Christ risen, and then to pass on our joy to others.

It should be easy for us also to find joy in the joy of Christ's Mother, who shared so intimately His suffering. If we have a bit of imagination, it is heart-warming to look in reverently on Jesus' visit with His Mother after the resurrection. As St. Ignatius, who suggests this contemplation, tells us, though this is not recorded in the Scriptures, only the dull of understanding would doubt that Jesus did visit His Mother.

We might picture Mary, risen early in the morning after a restless night haunted by horrors branded in her memory, with tracings of sorrow still on her face now turned to the first light of dawn. She prays with parts of psalms that have become favorites. In her heart the sharp pain of what had been, struggles with the hope of what was yet to be. For she recalls the annunciation message,...*reign will be without end,*[2] and the final words of Isaiah after he had so vividly shown the sufferings of the suffering servant:

> *...he shall see the light in fullness of days*[3]

Suddenly she senses a presence in the room, turns, and there is the glorified Jesus! As great as was her sorrow, now is her joy.

It could have been said of her before,

> *What example can I show you for your comfort,*
> *virgin daughter Zion?*
> *For great as the sea is your downfall;*
> *who can heal you?*[4]

Now she is comforted beyond expression. Great as the sea—she is inundated with consolation, ecstatic joy.

> Queen of heaven, rejoice! Alleluia!
> for He whom you were made worthy to bear
> is risen again, as He said. Alleluia!

1. Entrance antiphon
2. Lk. 1:33
3. Is. 53:11
4. Lam. 2:13

Second Sunday of Easter

Read 1 Pt. 1:3-9
Jn. 20:19-31
(A, B)

## I Rejoice in Your Inheritance

Imagine you have just been informed that you have come into a large inheritance. You are about to receive the means of realizing your wildest, most extravagant dreams. You see possibilities of action, enjoyment, fulfillment that make your heart leap with joy of anticipation. A whole new life opens before you.

Idle dreaming? You have in fact received an inheritance and the possibility of a new life that far surpasses anything experienced or imagined. We learned of this glorious prospect on Easter when we first heard the happy cry of "Alleluia!"—heard that Jesus Christ, our Savior and Leader, had broken the grip of death and emerged from the tomb to new life.

On this second Sunday of Easter we hear Peter, witness of the resurrection, speak of our inheritance and the new life given us:

*Praised be the God and Father*
*of our Lord Jesus Christ,*
*he who in his great mercy*
*gave us a new birth;*
*a birth unto hope which draws its life*

*from the resurrection of Jesus Christ from the dead;*
*a birth to an imperishable inheritance,*
*incapable of fading or defilement,*
*which is kept in heaven for you....*[1]

Another witness, the beloved John who had shared deeply the pain and shame of the crucifixion, adds his reason for our trust in the inheritance: that we are *children* of God through faith.

*Everyone who believes that Jesus is the Christ has been begotten of God....*[2]

"Everyone who believes": the Gospel shows us Thomas, who refused to believe without further evidence and on his own terms, and was in danger of losing everything. But Jesus pursued him.

*"...Take your finger and examine my hands. Put your hand into my side. Do not persist in your unbelief but believe!" Thomas said in response, "My Lord and my God!"*[3]

## II Wait for It in Patience

So the inheritance and the new life are for those who believe—and also understand those wounds which the Lord chose to keep even in His renewed body. It is for the followers who see they could hardly be called such if they themselves had never been marked by pain of body and spirit.

Peter also tells us to expect troubles but not to let them overcome our joy.

*There is cause for rejoicing here. You may for a time have to suffer the distress of many trials; but this is so that your faith, which is more precious than the passing splendor of fire-tried gold, may...lead to praise, glory and honor....*[4]

Peter's words of praise for those to whom he writes, because they have believed and loved the Lord without seeing Him, parallel those of Jesus to Thomas.

We must be patient in our anticipation of the inheritance, but we are also allowed a kind of happy carelessness, a spendthrift attitude, in our present life. With such an inheritance awaiting us, why should we worry about spending what we have, and ourselves also, in service to others? Why be sad at seeing youthful beauty and strength fade, or our health somewhat threatened, because of hard work? With St. Paul, we can even be glad to spend what we have and our own selves in service of the Lord, for part of the inheritance is a gloriously renewed body.

If the Holy Spirit has given us some appreciation of what it means to be God's children and to possess the inheritance we have through Christ, we shall delight in repeating the psalm response that runs through this liturgy:

*Give thanks to the Lord, for he is good,*
*for his mercy endures forever.*[5]

1. 1 Pt. 1:3-4 (second reading, A)
2. 1 Jn. 5:1 (second reading, B)
3. Jn. 20:27-28 (Gospel, B)
4. 1 Pt. 1:6-7 (second reading, A)
5. Ps. 118: 1

## Third Sunday of Easter

Read Lk. 24:13-48
(A, B)

# I Uncertain Vision

In the various accounts of the appearances of our Lord after His resurrection a striking feature is the element of obscurity.The disciples knew that it was Jesus, yet His appearance in this new state did not allow them entire certainty from simple sight. In the story of Emmaus, we see two disciples trudging along, sadly recalling the events of Christ's death and burial. Then,

> *In the course of their lively exchange, Jesus approached and began to walk along with them. However, they were restrained from recognizing him.*[1]

In the sequel, when they had returned to Jerusalem and joined the other disciples, Jesus was suddenly standing among them. Again there was some uncertainty, and alarm, in spite of His greeting, *"Peace to you!"*

> *In their panic and fright they thought they were seeing a ghost. He said to them, "Why are you disturbed? Why do such ideas cross your mind?"*[2]

Again, in the climactic ending of Matthew's Gospel, Jesus appears in Galilee, in a prearranged meeting. Even with this expectancy, there had been doubts:

> *At the sight of him, those who had entertained doubts fell down in homage.*[3]

## II Confirmation in Signs

Although the disciples could not rely entirely on evidence of sight, they knew Jesus through familiar words and signs. When those of the Emmaus episode returned to Jerusalem,

> *...they recounted what had happened on the road and how they had come to know him in the breaking of the bread.*[4]

These two were not of the eleven who certainly witnessed the institution of the Eucharist. This action of Jesus at Emmaus may have been the Eucharist, but perhaps this breaking of bread, aside from the Eucharist, had already become a familiar gesture of love and sharing in the Christian community in process of formation when the disciples were going about with the Lord. *We* are fortunate to know Him in the breaking of bread through which He shares Himself, even in His divinity, and makes a community that is one body, living a divine life.

When the disciples in the upper room in Jerusalem thought they were seeing a ghost, they were invited to go beyond appearances and to touch those signs of His love, the wounds in His hands and feet.

> *Touch me, and see that a ghost does not have flesh and bones....*[5]

For us, too, these enduring wounds are signs, accepted from the Gospel witness, through which we arrive with a marveling joy at that *faith in the Son of God who loved me and gave himself for me.*[6]

## III Joy in God's Word

Through the Scriptures we come to know God and His Son Jesus. It is not necessary, or enough, to know them as a Scripture scholar might know them if he does not combine prayer with his study. Meditating on the word with reverence, desiring to know interiorly—to taste, as St. Ignatius puts it—we may arrive at a deep joy in the communication of God with men.

> *Were not our hearts burning inside us as he talked to us on the road and explained the Scriptures to us?*[7]

> *Then he opened their minds to the understanding of the Scriptures.... "You are witnesses...."*[8]

This is part of our Christian joy, that He opens our minds to understand His word; and that He sends us to be witnesses of the Good News that is the world's joy.

> Alleluia!
> Lord Jesus make your word plain to us,
> make our hearts burn with love when you speak.
> Alleluia![9]

1. Lk. 24:15-16 (Gospel, A)
2. Lk. 24:36-37 (Gospel, B)
3. Mt. 28:17
4. Lk. 24:35
5. Lk. 24:39
6. Gal. 2:20
7. Lk. 24:32 (Gospel, A)
8. Lk. 24:45, 48 (Gospel, B)
9. Gospel acclamation

*Why are you disturbed?... Look at my hands and feet; it is really I.*[1]

Pierced hands they were that guided me
through childhood's nascent years.
Pierced hands chastised youth's waywardness—
then wiped away the tears.

Pierced hands that beckoned, led away
the ones I loved as life,
that soothed the throbbing hurt where first
they used the cleaving knife.

Pierced hands implore, urge on, restrain,
as recklessly I roam;
the same strong, gentle hands of God
at last shall lead me home.

1. Lk. 24:38-39

## Fourth Sunday of Easter

Read Ps. 23
Jn. 10:11-18
(A, B, C)

*The Lord is my shepherd; I shall not want.*
*In verdant pastures he gives me repose;*
*Beside restful waters he leads me;*
*he refreshes my soul.*[1]

Clean sheep in lush green pastures
eating together, resting on soft sward,
are secure in the flocking.

But always the restless one,
looking to where goats on the crags
bleat their contempt for
the herded and led.

So, straying, picking at whim
a way to the heady heights,
rising to challenge of wild wind
and glistening, barren peak.

Then waning light and weariness.
Tasting the berried browse, finding it
honey on tongue but burning in belly.

Wrapped in lonely shroud of night,
cringing at cry of predator,
shaking in chill of thin air.

Suddenly a familiar footstep,
the assuring voice;
a gathering into strong arms
against the warm breast.
In swinging light, a flash
of the Shepherd's sweated brow
and bleeding hands.

*Yet it was I...*
*who took them in my arms;*
*I drew them with human cords,*
*with bonds of love;*
*I fostered them like one*
*who raises an infant to his cheeks;*
*Yet, though I stooped to feed my child,*
*they did not know that I was their healer.*[2]

*I am the good shepherd:*
*the good shepherd lays down his life for the sheep.*[3]

1. Ps. 23:1-3 (responsorial psalm, A)
2. Hos. 11:3-4
3. Jn. 10:11 (Gospel, B)

## Fifth Sunday of Easter

Read Jn. 14:1-12
1 Jn. 3:18-24
(A, C)

# I Seeing the Father

*Whoever has seen me has seen the Father.*[1]

Jesus is revealed gradually through the Holy Spirit, especially as we meditate on the Sacred Scriptures. Faith searches for Him continually, driven on by love. Gradually we gain new insights; and we do not grow weary in the quest because we have accepted the remarkable words of Jesus,

*I am the Way, and the Truth, and the Life.*[2]

These words lead us to say with the temple police who had been sent by the Pharisees to arrest Jesus, *No man ever spoke like that before.*[3] His words express His identity, for there never *was* a man like this. He dares to say,

*If you really knew me, you would know my*
*Father also....*
*I am in the Father*
*and the Father is in me.*[4]

*I am the Way.* Help us, Lord. You, as Way, are not so inviting to our broken nature. There is a broader way, a smoother way, with a wide entrance. Help us to remember that it leads to destruction. It is when You join us as You joined the disciples on the way to Emmaus that Your way becomes easy, that we walk with energy, our hearts burning within us as You reveal Yourself. You show us how fitting it is that the Messiah should suffer and so enter into His glory,[5] and that we should follow in suffering to glory.

## II Believing and Loving

*I am the Truth.* Lord, we do not learn this easily from our television, movies, newspapers and magazines. Your voice in our world is such a quiet one, and who is listening? Who will cloister his mind in silence that he may hear You? And when he does listen, will he find a babble—even in the voices in Your Church—that tempts him to adopt Pilate's cynical question,

> *"Truth... What does that mean?"*[6]

Send us Your Spirit, to give *knowledge* of those essentials which Your Church certainly holds to, *wisdom* to choose our way where a justifiable uncertainty has opened divergent paths, and *fortitude* to bear the pains of our lost security and our fears of being misled. Even when it seems to be twilight, we trust that when we follow after You we will not walk in darkness, for You are the Light of life.

> *His commandment is this:*
> *we are to believe in the name of his Son, Jesus Christ,*
> *and are to love one another as he commanded us.*[7]

## III Renewing Creation

Faith must issue in practical love:

*...let us love in deed and in truth*
*and not merely talk about it.*[8]

The Gospel and the second reading for Cycle C significantly relate a *new* commandment and a *new* heaven and earth. The measure in which Christ's "new" commandment of love permeates the human family will be the measure of progress toward the final renewal of the earth.

*I give you a new commandment:*
*Love one another.*[9]

*Then I saw new heavens and a new earth; the former heavens and the former earth had passed away.... I saw...the holy city...beautiful as a bride prepared to meet her husband.... This is God's dwelling among men.*[10]

1. Jn. 14:9 (Gospel, A)
2. Jn. 14:6
3. Jn. 7:46
4. Jn. 14:7, 10
5. cf. Lk. 24:26
6. Jn. 18:38
7. 1 Jn. 3:23 (second reading, B)
8. 1 Jn. 3:18
9. Jn. 13:34
10. Rv. 21:1-3

## Sixth Sunday of Easter

Read Acts 15:1-2, 22-29
Jn. 14:15-29
(B, C)

# I Gift of the Spirit

In the first readings for Cycles A and B we have two incidents from Acts which show the freedom of the Holy Spirit. In Samaria the people accepted the word and were baptized; then Peter and John went and laid hands on them and they received the Holy Spirit. In Caesarea Peter and the believers with him were astonished to see the Spirit come upon the pagans to whom Peter had preached. These were baptized *after* receiving the Spirit.

> *The wind blows where it will.*
> *...you do not know where it comes from,*
> *or where it goes.*
> *So it is with everyone begotten of the Spirit.*[1]

The Spirit is not the exclusive possession of the Catholic Church, which some may have tended in times past to believe. As Vatican II tells us,[2] those who do not belong to the visible Catholic Church but believe in Christ and have been baptized, are joined with that Church in the Holy Spirit, who manifests among men His power and gifts. And those who do not know Christ and His Church are still drawn by the Spirit toward the unity and fullness of life enjoyed by the People of God.

Peter confesses,

> *I begin to see how true it is that God shows no partiality. Rather, the man of any nation who fears God and acts uprightly is acceptable to him.*

The Spirit of Love is poured out in a divine impulsiveness:

> *Peter had not finished these words when the Holy Spirit descended upon all who were listening....*[3]

## II Love

The Gospels for all three sets of readings for this Sunday draw from Christ's discourse on the evening before His death. It is a revelation of His heart's love, asking love in return. It reveals the nature of true Christian love.

LOVE IS FREE. We have today a new emphasis on freedom, responsibility and the motive of love. Even in apostolic times, when some believers wished to oblige pagan converts to the law of Moses and circumcision, we are given an early model of communal discernment, prayerful discussion and authoritative decision:

> *It is the decision of the Holy Spirit, and ours too, not to lay on you any burden beyond that which is strictly necessary....*[4]

Augustine's "Love and then do as you will" is valid because one who loves deeply is pleased only with what pleases the loved one.

*Anyone who loves me*
*will be true to my word....*[5]

LOVE IS OBEDIENT.

*You will live in my love*
*if you keep my commandments,*
*Even as I have kept my Father's commandments,*
*and live in his love.*[6]

From these words of Christ, the necessity for obedience is obvious. The central Christian belief in Christ's suffering, dying and rising for the salvation of men would be meaningless if the necessity of obedience were rejected. In the Garden, in His agony and revulsion at the suffering about to engulf Him, He prays,...*yet not my will but yours be done.*[7] Submitting our wills to God is the only way to the eternal life of love. There can only be question of how that will is best discerned.

LOVE IS SELF-SACRIFICING. Christ's love for us was unto death.

*There is no greater love than this:*
*to lay down one's life for one's friends.*[8]

And then He asks of us—self-centered, envious, ambitious, insensitive to others' needs—that we

*love one another*
*as I have loved you.*[9]

LOVE IS GLAD AT THE JOY OF OTHERS. We should
*rejoice with those who rejoice, weep with those who weep.*[10]
*If you truly loved me you would rejoice to have me go to the Father....*[11]

God lives in the soul that loves.

*...my Father will love him;*
*we will come to him*
*and make our dwelling place with him.*[12]

"Come, Holy Spirit! Kindle the fire of Your love!"

1. Jn. 3:8
2. Cf. The Church, 15-16
3. Acts 10:34-35, 44 (first reading, B)
4. Cf. Acts 15:28 (first reading, C)
5. Jn. 14:23 (Gospel, C)
6. Jn. 15:10 (Gospel, B)
7. Lk. 22:42
8. Jn. 15:13
9. Jn. 15:12
10. Rom. 12:15
11. Jn. 14:28 (Gospel, C)
12. Jn. 14:23

## Ascension

Read Acts 1:1-11
Eph. 1:17-23

# I Looking Up

*Shout joyfully to God, all you on earth,*
*sing praise to the glory of his name;*
*proclaim his glorious praise.*
*Say to God, "How tremendous are your deeds!"*[1]

Man's first daring exploration beyond the gravitational influence of the earth, into moon orbit, and back again to earth, gave us not only a very close look at the moon, but perhaps more significantly, a new look at our earth.

This blue-and-white marble moving through the black expanses of space: what is it doing out there? What is its significance, when we know its small size and cramped orbit in the vastness measured by "light years" which have no practical relation to the rules and measures that suffice on our little ball?

Photographs of the earth from near the moon impress and crystalize what we had come to realize: how small a world we live in, what a compact unity of life it is that like a gossamer net encircles the crust of this third planet from the sun in one of the lesser systems of the universe.

In this amazing new perspective, man really saw the earth, his home, for the first time. One of the astronauts, fascinated by the sight of our globe from a quarter of a million miles distance, was struck by the thought that a space traveler from another planet might have looked at the earth and never guessed there was life there; but if there was, he would think how inextricably interwoven would have to be the lives and destiny of any inhabitants on this isolated globe.

That thin layer of life on the surface of the earth is something far greater than biological. In the pre-history of the planet *darkness covered the abyss, while a mighty wind swept the waters.*[2] In its recent history God's Son walked upon the earth to dispel the darkness, then sent the Spirit of God to renew, integrate, and make divine its human life.

## II Alpha and Omega

*I am the Alpha and the Omega....*[3]

The Lord is Beginning and End, source of all creation and its goal. Jesus is the Head of His Church, that body to which we belong, and He

> *has made us a royal nation of priests in the service of his God and Father....*[4]

We are kings, rulers of creation, priests, who together with our great High Priest consecrate the universe to God. It is the love of the Son of God, uniting all the love of the human family and going out to the Father in a song of praise, that makes this bright blue-and-white marble unique among the countless shining bodies that fill the heavens. The Father

> *has put all things under Christ's feet and has made him, thus exalted, head of the church, which is his body: the fullness of him who fills the universe in all its parts.*[5]

> *God has given us the wisdom to understand fully the mystery, the plan he was pleased to decree in Christ, to be carried out in the fullness of time: namely, to bring all things in the heavens and on earth into one under Christ's headship.... In him we were chosen....*[6]

On this feast of the Ascension we look up to where Christ has gone to be with His Father, and with Mary and the apostles, we long to be with Him. But, "Why are you standing here...?" We have work to do. *Go...make disciples of all the nations.* Make known to all men their Lord and Redeemer, and His Father, Ruler of the universe.

> *All you peoples, clap your hands,*
> *shout to God with cries of gladness,*
> *For the Lord, the Most High, the awesome,*
> *is the great king over all the earth.*[7]

1. Ps. 66:1-3
2. Gn. 1:2
3. Rv. 1:8
4. Rv. 1:6
5. Eph. 1:22-23 (second reading)
6. Eph. 1:9-11
7. Ps. 47:2-3 (responsorial psalm)

# Seventh Sunday of Easter

Read Jn. 17:1-26
(B, C)

## I Chosen Out of the World

The Gospel readings for the three cycles of this Sunday give us consecutively the seventeenth chapter of St. John in which he reports at length the prayer of Christ for His apostles on the evening of the Eucharistic banquet, just before His suffering and death. In this atmosphere of intimacy, of leave-taking, and of apprehension of what would happen to these His chosen ones, He pours out His love and His desires for them. The more to impress upon them His personal, selective love, He seems to be excluding others.

> *I have made your name known*
> *to those you gave me out of the world....*
> *For these I pray—*
> *not for the world....*[1]
>
> *I do not ask you to take them out of the world,*
> *but to guard them from the evil one.*
> *They are not of the world,*
> *any more than I belong to the world.*[2]

Standing alone, these words of Christ could be interpreted to mean: "Let us abhor the world. We are the lucky, chosen ones; let us preserve our status by avoiding contact with the world." This interpretation, however, points up the necessity for wide reading of and meditation on the Scriptures, a sustained effort to learn the whole Christ; to pray over the ubiquitous paradoxes, to balance the apparent contradictions. Here we distinguish between two meanings of "the world," that world created by a God who "saw that it was good," and the sinful, seductive world of men alienated from their Maker and opposed to Christ. Let us humbly pray to the Holy Spirit for that true knowledge of our Lord Jesus Christ which the learned Paul prized above all:

> *I wish to know Christ and the power flowing from his resurrection; likewise to know how to share in his sufferings....*[3]

## II Calling All Creation

Even in His prayer for the select few, Christ's heart could not refrain from reaching out to others.

> *I do not pray for them alone.*
> *I pray also for those who will believe in me through their word....*[4]

But it was after the gift of the Holy Spirit to the infant Church that the whole wide world, every human person, knew the choosing of God's love, the only love that can be both jealously individual and universal. As He was leaving the earth to go to His Father, the Lord dissolved all the seeming exclusiveness of His choosing to salvation and life:

> *Go into the whole world and proclaim the good news to all creation. The man who believes in it and accepts baptism will be saved....*[5]

*See, I send down upon you the promise of my Father. Remain here in the city until you are clothed with power from on high.*[6]

Although in His brief public life Christ continually went about doing good and proclaiming the Good News, He limited Himself to a small section of humanity: *My mission is only to the lost sheep of the house of Israel.*[7] But He asked His apostles to go into the whole world—in the power of the Spirit.

*...No one who comes to me will I ever reject.*[8]

I come to You, Lord, knowing my unfitness to be chosen, yet in complete confidence. But Lord, there are so many others needing to be chosen, who search for You restlessly, sometimes unknowingly; so many thirsty souls in this beautiful garden of the world which proves for them a mirage in the desert. Open up a way for me to help bring them to Your fountains, to realize Your promise:

*The afflicted and the needy seek water in vain....*
*I, the Lord, will answer them;*
*I, the God of Israel, will not forsake them.*
*I will open up rivers on the bare heights,*
*and fountains in the broad valleys;*
*I will turn the desert into a marshland,*
*and the dry ground into springs of water.*[9]

*Let him who is thirsty come forward; let all who desire it accept the gift of life-giving water.*[10]

1. Jn. 17:6, 9 (Gospel, A)
2. Jn. 17:15-16 (Gospel, B)
3. Phil. 3:10
4. Jn. 17:20 (Gospel, C)
5. Mk. 16:15-16
6. Lk. 24:49
7. Mt. 15:24
8. Jn. 6:37
9. Is. 41:17-18
10. Rv. 22:17 (second reading, C)

Pentecost

Read Acts 2:1-11

# I Tongues of Fire

The tongue which can ignite the fire of love in others is the tongue set on fire by the Holy Spirit. This fire diffuses itself, spreads from heart to heart, a steady, warming, comforting flame. At times it is perhaps not so comforting, for it is also an antiseptic flame which can cause pain in the burning out of our sins and self-preoccupation.

This fire of the Spirit is a clean flame by which we see ourselves and others and all our surroundings clearly and in correct relationship: a light of knowledge and understanding and wisdom.

Every human heart really alive will generate fire. If it has rejected the Holy Spirit, it will burn with the uncontrollable, destructive fires of total self-serving, antagonisms, and sometimes hate. This fire is dark and smoky, obscuring the heavens and the sun-bathed mountain tops that challenge the human spirit.

*I am the light of the world.*
*No follower of mine shall ever walk in darkness;*
*no, he shall possess the light of life.*[1]

Jesus speaks thus of Himself. But He has ascended into heaven and rejoined the Father. Although we know He is still present among us and in us, He has indicated that a special, abiding presence of the Holy Spirit was necessary. This Spirit is sent by Jesus and the Father to make alive and immediate to us all the words of Jesus by which we must live.

*...the Holy Spirit*
*whom the Father will send in my name,*
*will instruct you in everything,*
*and remind you of all that I told you.*[2]

*It is much better for you that I go.*
*If I fail to go,*
*the Paraclete will never come to you...*
*...he will give glory to me,*
*because he will have received from me*
*what he will announce to you.*[3]

Come, Holy Spirit, come!
And from Your celestial home
Shed a ray of light divine!

Come, Father of the poor!
Come, source of all our store!
Come, within our bosoms shine![4]

## II Renew the Face of the Earth!

Our world is changing rapidly and drastically. We see fires burning everywhere. According to our age, background, temperament, possibly our insight, our individual opinions vary greatly as to the degree to which these many fires are simply destructive, or cleansing and renewing. Undoubtedly there is a mixture of these processes. Even as flames of destruction are widespread, so also the purifying and enlightening fires kindled by the Holy Spirit. Ours are times for testing economic, political and social structures under which many of us were so comfortable while others were very uncomfortable and oppressed. They are times of pain, uncertainty, and fear because some question even our basic beliefs and accepted moral standards.

These must be times of Christian faith and hope and action. The Holy Spirit is still among the people of God, a light to direct them, a fire to purify and weld into unity of divine love all of humanity, for the glorification of the Father.

> Lord, send out your Spirit,
> and renew the face of the earth.[5]
> Alleluia!
> Come, Holy Spirit, fill the hearts of your faithful;
> and kindle in them the fire of your love.
> Alleluia![6]

1. Jn. 8:12
2. Jn. 14:26
3. Jn. 16:7,14
4. Sequence
5. Responsorial antiphon
6. Gospel acclamation

## Second Sunday of the Year

Read Jn. 2:1-12
(C)

# I Sharing Gifts

*There are different gifts but the same Spirit; there are different ministries but the same Lord; there are different works but the same God who accomplishes all of them in everyone. To each person the manifestation of the Spirit is given for the common good.*[1]

We are to use our own particular gifts, of whatever kind and in whatever measure we possess them, for the good of the Christian community. The sharing with each other of the gifts we have—and each has something special to share—increases respect and love in the community, whether it be the community of the home, the parish, the neighborhood, or a larger group.

Sincere, open *dialogue,* in which all are delicately sensitive to the opinions, reactions, and feelings of others—and above all, truly willing to listen—can be an enriching as well as a conciliating experience. We begin to see what a diversity of gifts is possessed by the *community.*

Have we ever marveled at the unique character of each person? That we have never seen two human faces exactly alike, even in "identical" twins? That we can often recognize an individual by his walk, his laughter? That even such seemingly unimportant characteristics as finger prints are never the same? Then when we look to the faculties of intellect, memory and imagination, individual differences are even more remarkable.

If you should happen to be the parent of a large family, what striking differences you have noted in your children, though each has received from common parents a like hereditary legacy.

Spontaneous *group prayer* may impress upon us that the gifts of the Holy Spirit to individuals may be as diverse as their natural gifts. In prayer, too, the gifts we ourselves possess may be recognized, without exaggeration, without self-depreciation. By our sharing of these gifts, the community is greatly enriched.

## II In Community of Love

The Gospel (C) shows us Mary at a marriage, a community celebration of human love.[2]

O Mary, Mother of our Lord, we come to you to learn about love in a Christian community. When God, the Father of us all, sent us His Son, Jesus, who is our Life, you were asked to be His Mother. And so you became our Mother, too. You were the heart of that first small beginning of Christian community in the home at Nazareth. Or if the first true Christian community was the group of the apostles, you were there among them.

When Jesus began His public ministry for men in Cana, you were there. And it was such a human, communitarian celebration where He first showed His power and His love for men. We thought, Blessed Mother, He was saying to you, "This shortage of wine is no concern of mine"; that He was telling you He had come as Teacher, as Prophet, as the great High Priest, holy, set apart, somewhere between heaven and earth. But you knew His heart, and so you said to the waiters, "Do what he tells you." He used His divine power to save the embarrassment of a bride and groom and the joy of a celebration of life.

Then, at the end, you stood by the cross of your tortured Son, with that remnant of His community that was able to share deeply in the suffering that was to save and to make all one.

O Mother, say for us to Jesus, "They have no wine." We have only water, in earthen pots. Ask Him to make it the wine of love, which warms the inner self, releases our selfish inhibitions and leads us to share joy with others; which can even inebriate us with joy as we join together in the celebration of the new life in Jesus.

1. 1 Cor. 12:4-7 (second reading, C)
2. Cf. Jn. 2:1-12 (Gospel, C)

## Third Sunday of the Year

Read Jon. 3:1-5, 10
Mk. 1:14-20
(B)

### I Nirvana

Is this what Paul holds up to Christians as an ideal: a state of quiet, in separation from the external world, attained through suppression of desires and emotions?

> *...those with wives should live as though they had none; those who weep should live as though they were not weeping, and those who rejoice as though they were not rejoicing; buyers should conduct themselves as though they owned nothing....*[1]

A superficial glance may see some resemblance between the Buddhist nirvana and the Christian state of detachment. The Christian must aim at a certain tranquillity of spirit and freedom from external things: a fundamental attitude that St. Ignatius Loyola put at the very beginning of his *Spiritual Exercises* as a first principle, and which was expressed as "indifference." Father Delmage in his translation expresses it as the cultivation of "a free and independent attitude toward anything less than God or the cause of God or the promptings of the Holy Spirit regarding Christ in His members."[2] But it is a discipline in the use of things, situations and persons *in order to possess a joyful and effective freedom to live the Christian life.*

## II The Time Is Short[3]

Does this statement of Paul strengthen the impression that he is saying, "Withdraw and pay little attention to the world about you"? He adds, *the world as we know it is passing away.*

In a sense all of us are aware that the world as we know it is passing away. In the rapid change in all about us, we seem incapable of keeping in step with our world. There must be discouragement and frustration at times for many of us:

> The scientist, technologist and scholar trying to keep abreast of new discoveries, techniques, materials and methods that are so constantly developing.
>
> The physician or psychiatrist, often weary from taking care of an overload of patients and unable to spend the time he needs to study the new in his field.
>
> The teacher of certain disciplines, unsure that what he teaches now will be acceptable next year.
>
> And the ordinary Christian who does not have the time—and possibly the ability or background—to consider and judge the new in his changing Church, and so feels uncertain and confused.

So, even if we are young and healthy and have no fear of passing soon from this world through death, it is still true that the world as we know it today is quickly passing away. Should we resign from our society, withdraw from the race? Paul's last directive is, *...make use of the world* (and who does not?) *as though...not using it.* We must not become engrossed in it.

St. Paul needed to oppose the philosophy of some of his Corinthians, *"Let us eat and drink, for tomorrow we die!"*[4] A popular song of some years ago expressed it, "Enjoy yourself, it's later than you think"; and much of our advertising has something of the same spirit.

## III Up! Go!

The first reading and Gospel seem to contrast with the second reading in that they demand *involvement.* But the very fact that the "time is growing short" demands action because Christian life is always apostolic.

Jonah is pressed by the Lord to go to Nineveh because its time is short.

> *"Set out for the great city of Nineveh, and announce to it the message that I will tell you." "...Forty days more and Nineveh shall be destroyed."*[5]

The threat was conditional. Nineveh was saved through the repentance of the people, to the chagrin of the prophet who expected literal fulfillment of his warning.

In the Gospel, Jesus gives what must have seemed a rather urgent invitation to follow Him and proclaim the Good News, for the men immediately leave their father and their work. *This is the time of fulfillment. The reign of God is at hand!*[6]

The word, then, for every Christian, no matter how indirect his spreading of the Good News, is *action* in his world; but with freedom springing from a disciplined choice and use of things, attained through prayerful discernment.

*Your ways, O Lord, make known to me;*
*teach me your paths.*[7]

1. 1 Cor. 7:29-30 (second reading, B)
2. Delmage, *Spiritual Exercises of St. Ignatius Loyola,* "Principle or Foundation."
3. 1 Cor. 7:29
4. 1 Cor. 15:32
5. Jon. 3:2, 4 (B)
6. Mk. 1:15 (B)
7. Ps. 25:4

## Fourth Sunday of the Year

Read Lk. 4:21-30
Mt. 5:1-12
1 Cor 13:4-13
(C, A, B)

# I Crucial Question

> *...who do you say that I am?*[1]

In the readings for cycles B and C for this Sunday we find a search for the identity of Jesus of Nazareth.

> *Is not this Joseph's son?*[2]

We know Him, His relatives, the circumstances of His quiet life in our little town. How does He dare relate Himself to the prophecies of Isaiah, to claim that the spirit of the Lord is given to Him in a special manner, that He is sent by God—to heal and free *them?* He is making out that they are being favored by fulfillment of prophecy as they listen to His words.

Jesus is accepted by some and praised:

> *All who were present spoke favorably of him; they marveled at the appealing discourse which came from his lips.*[3]

He was rejected and hated by some. At the end of His talk in the synagogue of His own town, the people are in a rage because He blames them for not receiving Him as a prophet. They are ready to throw Him over a cliff, but He slips away.

Jesus was probably unknown, or ignored, by the majority of the men of His world. But it was God's plan that the Light of the World should rise slowly and increase gradually until all the earth was bathed in it.

## II Developing Answers

In the first reading (B) Moses promises a prophet to speak for God because the people were afraid to receive a more direct communication.

> *Let us not again hear the voice of the Lord our God...lest we die.*[4]

We are told that the Lord approved these words and promised to speak through a prophet He would raise up, a man like themselves, a brother. The full and final answer to this request of the people is Jesus of Nazareth, combining in Himself both the authority of the God who appeared to Moses in fire and thunder on the mountain, and the lowliness of the small-town carpenter.

Jesus is accepted as a *prophet*, and as a *teacher* different from those they were accustomed to, who were interpreters of traditional teaching. He taught new things, and with authority.[5] But even John the Baptist, on the word of Jesus Himself, was more than just one of the prophets. And John says he is not worthy to unfasten the strap of Jesus' sandal.

Jesus is known as a *healer*, and one who can control "unclean spirits." Such a spirit cries out, *"I know who you are—the holy One of God!"*[6] Then, in reading the apostles John and Paul, we cannot doubt the claim for divinity of the man of Nazareth. This claim, like a giant electric billboard, forces itself upon us at many a turn on the dimly-lighted highway of our life.

## III Full Response

It is interesting that Paul and John, most explicit proponents of Jesus' divinity, are also most insistent about love, summation of God's revelation of Himself and of our response to Him.

In the Gospel for Cycle A, Jesus attaches a happiness to particular responses of that underlying, motivating love which is so beautifully praised in the second reading for Cycle C. The two readings complement each other.

| *Jesus:* | *Paul:* |
| --- | --- |
| *How blest are the poor in spirit.... Blest are they who show mercy....* | *Love is patient; love is kind...it does not put on airs....* *[Love] is not prone to anger; neither does it brood over injuries.* |
| *Blest are the single-hearted for they shall see God.* | *It is not self-seeking.... Now we see indistinctly, as in a mirror; then we shall see face to face.* |
| *Blest too the peacemakers....*[7] | *Love is not jealous... there is no limit to love's forbearance....*[8] |

Faith in Jesus as Lord requires this kind of love, which is ruinous to smug self-love. But we cannot escape the choice, the surrender.

*Come, let us bow down in worship;*
*let us kneel before the Lord who made us.*
*For he is our God....*

*Oh, that today you would hear his voice:*
*"Harden not your hearts...."*[9]

1. Mt. 16:15
2. Lk. 4:22 (Gospel, C)
3. Lk. 4:22
4. Dt. 18:16
5. Cf. Mk. 1:27 (Gospel, B)
6. Mk. 1:24 (Gospel, B)
7. Cf. Mt. 5:3-10
8. Cf. 1 Cor. 13:4-12
9. Ps. 95:6-8 (responsorial psalm, B)

## Fifth Sunday of the Year

Read Is. 6:1-8
Rv. 4:8-11
Mt. 5:13-16
(C)

### I Holiness of God and Fear

The natural reaction to a sense of God's holiness is fear and humility. Primitive peoples offered sacrifices to appease the anger of their gods. A basic "fear of the Lord" is necessary for Christians, but this is a filial fear and respect. It is accompanied by gratitude and trust, founded on the belief *that Christ died for our sins.*[1] When reverence for God's holiness has brought us to keep His commandments, He leads us to a grateful love.

> *I will worship...*
> *and give thanks to your name,*
> *Because of your kindness and your truth....*
> *When I called, you answered me;*
> *you built up strength within me.*[2]

In the *Spiritual Exercises* of St. Ignatius, we are asked to begin the retreat by placing ourselves before our Creator in a spirit of fear, reverence and humility, looking on all the creatures that surround us as gifts at our disposal, but to be used in a manner suitable to a sinner. Because of our disordered desires we must deal with all things in a spirit of abnegation—ready to say "no" to those desires, choosing only what our discernment finds more useful towards the end for which we were created. There is here a basic "fear of the Lord" proper to one who realizes his sinfulness. Then passing on to the specific consideration of our sins, we are directed to place ourselves again in the midst of the whole array of creation, and to ask, to wonder, why all this has been placed at *our* service when *we* have failed to properly serve our Creator.

At the end of our retreat, having experienced our redemption through Christ's death and resurrection, and asking to be filled with grateful love, we place ourselves once more in the presence of the whole of creation. Now we are to see it more in sentiments of joy at its good rather than fear of its power of seduction. One who is purified and strengthened with grace views the universe with unselfish delight and uses its blessings with greater freedom. Gratitude and love are the proper response here, but there is still an element of fear, of awe and reverence, because we are to see God Himself working in all creatures, giving them being and life. We are to look upon God's gifts to us as a sign of His desire to give even Himself as far as He can.

## II Apostolic Humility

In the first reading (C) Isaiah professes he is wretched, unclean and unworthy to do God's work. A burning coal is touched to his mouth to purge him and give effectiveness to his words. A prophet is given God's message for the people and power to help them only after his own acknowledgment of sinfulness and God's merciful purification.

Paul is moved to say, *I am the least of the apostles,*[3] but he becomes the most profound expositor of Christ's redemptive death and resurrection.

Peter makes his confession, *Leave me, Lord. I am a sinful man;* but Christ assures him that he is chosen to *catch men.*[4] He will again show his all-too-human weakness in his denial of Christ at the accusation of a servant girl; then deep sorrow, and he is reaffirmed as chief of the apostles, the stand-in for the Good Shepherd to feed His lambs and sheep.

> *...I have prayed for you, that your faith may never fail. You in your turn must strengthen your brothers.*[5]

This is a consoling word for the apostolic man who sees himself weak and often failing. He has assurance that Christ prays particularly for him too, and strengthens him that he may strengthen his brothers.

Humility is never a self-depreciation that professes it has nothing to give. In the gospel for Cycle A we are admonished to be the light of the world, for God's glory.

> *...your light must shine before men so that they may see goodness in your acts and give praise to your heavenly Father.*[6]

For lack of eloquence, of scriptural and theological knowledge, we may be diffident about our being a light through our words. However, Paul says he does not rely on oratory or philosophical arguments, but simple presentation of Christ crucified. Even if our words are not a shining light, our good works must be:

*Sharing your bread with the hungry,*
*sheltering the oppressed and the homeless;*
*Clothing the naked....*[7]

1. 1 Cor. 15:3 (second reading, C)
2. Ps. 138:2-3 (responsorial psalm, C)
3. 1 Cor. 15:9 (second reading, C)
4. Cf. Lk. 5:1-11 (Gospel, C)
5. Lk. 22:32
6. Mt. 5:16
7. Is. 58:7 (first reading, A)

## Sixth Sunday of the Year

Read Mk. 1:40-45
(B)

# I The Horror of Leprosy

We are shocked when we consider the humiliation and loneliness of a leper under the law of Moses.

> *"The one who bears the sore of leprosy shall keep his garments rent and his head bare, and shall muffle his beard; he shall cry out, 'Unclean, unclean!' As long as the sore is on him he shall declare himself unclean.... He shall dwell apart, making his abode outside the camp."*[1]

Suppose a *sinner* were treated like this today. In many ways the spiritual disorder of serious sin resembles the physical evil of leprosy: it may be, though not always, a deformity that is repulsive to others; it makes us in effect, though not visibly, outcasts from the community of the Church; it weakens, incapacitates and brings death.

In the early Church one whose serious sin was public was treated somewhat as a leper was in the Old Law. He was separated from the community and subjected to a period of public penance. We live in more tolerant times, as is obvious if we compare this treatment of sinners with the "penance" *we* generally do after confession of sins! We have seen Jesus healing leprosy and other diseases upon a simple request in humility and faith. And we have seen that He wipes out sin as easily as bodily disease.

> *"Have courage, son, your sins are forgiven!" "...To help you realize that the Son of Man has authority on earth to forgive sins,"—he then said to the paralyzed man—"Stand up! Roll up your mat, and go home."*[2]

In the Gospel we see the faith of a man requesting restoration to health. It is the same faith we must have for the healing of our souls.

> *"If you will to do so, you can cure me." "...I will do it. Be cured."*[3]

It is as simple as that for us today. Always He wants to heal, waits for our sincere desire for it. He imposes on us the same easily fulfilled condition:

> *...Go off and present yourself to the priest....*[4]

## II The Joy of a Cure

In the recently restored communal penance service, we have, as in the early Church, an external expression of restoration to the honor and love shared by the community of the Church, the Body of Christ, which cannot have any leprous members intimately united to it.

Surely most of us who have been accustomed to receive the sacrament of reconciliation have at times deeply experienced the joy and peace that come from the definite assurance of being forgiven and restored to spiritual vigor. It is part of the joy of the resurrection message, for we heard the Lord say

*"Peace be with you...."*
*"As the Father has sent me,*
*so I send you....*
*If you forgive men's sins,*
*they are forgiven them...."*[5]

In the responsorial psalm, we sing with "the joy of salvation" which follows confession of our faults. We are cured, forgiven; taken back to the full rich life of the community of Christ.

*Happy is he whose fault is taken away....*
*Then I acknowledged my sin to you,*
*my guilt I covered not,*
*I said, "I confess my faults to the Lord...."*

*Be glad in the Lord and rejoice, you just;*
*exult, all you upright of heart.*[6]

1. Lv. 13:45-46 (first reading, B)
2. Mt. 9:2-6
3. Mk. 1:40-41 (Gospel, B)
4. Mk. 1:44
5. Jn. 20:21, 23
6. Ps. 32:1, 5, 11

## Seventh Sunday of the Year

Read Lk. 6:27-38
(C)

# I Radical Demands

*To you who hear me, I say....*[1]

Lord, we want to listen to Your words, but You make it difficult. You are asking us deliberately to make ourselves a soft touch, a loser, a patsy. Our sense of justice and our dignity rebel at what You ask:

that we give without hope of receiving;
that we remain peaceable even in great provocation;
that we bear hurt and injustice without retaliation;
that we love when we are not loved in return.

Lord Jesus, teach us that our dignity is to be like You, who gave Yourself to humiliation and suffering; that mercy is above justice—as we must hope at the time of our own judgment. Through the Holy Spirit may we understand the thrust of Your words and have courage to follow them.

The radical ethical demands of Jesus will always be a source of uneasiness and pain to His serious followers.

*Love your enemies, do good to those who hate you; bless those who curse you and pray for those who maltreat you. When someone slaps you on one cheek, turn and give him the other....*[2]

We can make plausible excuses for submerging the more radical sayings of Jesus: He was using the oriental style of exaggeration and startling imagery; He was emphasizing the eschatological, the absolute necessity of ordering life to the final end, minimizing the practical demands of our everyday human living. But if we are sincere followers of Christ, these words of His are ideals we firmly cling to and try to practice whenever possible. Though these directions are not to be literally followed in every situation, they remain ideals by which we try to regulate our relationships with others—ideals ever in the background of our consciousness in individual decisions.

## II Balance of Hope and Fear

The desire for a guaranteed security is universal, as is witnessed by the wide acceptance of the necessity for life, health and property insurance. We may long for spiritual security, too, when we consider the greatness and holiness of God and our own insignificance and evil tendencies, our numerous failings in living up to Christian ideals. Our performance in the light of Jesus' demands to rise above the natural habit of loving only those who love us, of treating others as they treat us, may be a source of fear, but there is a reassuring balance of hope in the promises He attaches to some of His directives. He does offer security, a "life insurance," for which we must pay the premium of Christian love—a relationship with others that goes beyond simple equity.

> *Then will your recompense be great. You will rightly be called sons of the Most High.... Do not judge, and you will not be judged. Do not condemn, and you will not be condemned. Pardon, and you shall be pardoned. Give, and it shall be given to you. Good measure pressed down, shaken together, running over....*[3]

Jesus, thank You for these consoling words, for this spiritual life insurance. Not that we have always kept up with the premiums, fulfilled the conditions which justify such happy hopes, but we are trying—and You are very reluctant to cancel our policy. We fail so often, are so wanting in generosity, so often surprised by our hair-trigger impulses. Keep us determined to follow these counsels of Yours and confident in the promises You attach to them. Give us the strength to walk in Your ways.

> *By the Lord are the steps of a man made firm,*
> *and he approves his way.*
> *Though he fall, he does not lie prostrate,*
> *for the hand of the Lord sustains him.*[4]

1. Lk. 6:27
2. Lk. 6:27-29 (Gospel, C)
3. Lk. 6:35, 37-38 (Gospel, C)
4. Ps. 37:23-24

## Eighth Sunday of the Year

Read Ps. 103:1-13
Mt. 6:24-34
(B, A)

### I I Will Never Forget You

Loneliness, a feeling of abandonment, is surely one of the more painful of human vicissitudes. This isolating smog frequently settles upon the old, but it can choke the joy of life in the young also, and even in those who seem surrounded with friends and compatible companions. Man's spirit has its place of deep withdrawal, where others cannot follow, and where, if it does not find God present in some manner, it experiences the chill of naked aloneness, of unfulfilled needs. This pain can come upon the rich as well as the most needy, on the famous as well as the forgotten, on the sanguine and the extrovert as well as the melancholy and the introvert. The soul is an empty mold needing to be filled; a parched desert soil needing to be watered and wakened to life; a vacuum tense with the need of an equalizing, tranquilizing presence.

We should find relief to aching loneliness in the comforting words of the Scriptures. If I feel ignored, unappreciated, abandoned, or completely insignificant in the crowded, busy world, I can know from His word that God's fatherly love embraces me.

*As a father has compassion on his children,*
*so the Lord has compassion on those who fear him.*[1]
*Merciful and gracious is the Lord,*
*slow to anger and abounding in kindness....*
*Not according to our sins does he deal with us,*
*nor does he requite us according to our crimes.*[2]

His love for me is like the love of a mother for her son—no, it *exceeds* it.

*But Zion said, "The Lord has forsaken me;*
*my Lord has forgotten me."*
*Can a mother forget her infant,*
*be without tenderness for the child of her womb?*
*Even should she forget,*
*I will never forget you.*[3]

## II I Will Look After You

The Lord bids us to consider the birds in the sky and the flowers in the field, how God cares for them, and not to worry about our own needs.

*...will he not provide much more for you,*
*O weak in faith!*[4]

The awesome power of the advertising business may confuse in our minds our real basic needs with desires stimulated by psychological pressures. Jesus Christ does not promise that His Father's providence will provide all that Madison Avenue suggests is necessary for a happy life. In affluent America we are in danger of false expectations of providence; or of forgetting our dependence upon it; or of smug acceptance of every kind of luxury as God's blessings whereas they may be partly the result of international injustices for which we feel no personal guilt. On the other hand, how difficult may be this faith in providence for a man lying hungry and sick on a street in Calcutta, or a victim of fratricidal strife in Africa or northern Ireland. And what a sobering thought that in these instances we have evidence that man's injustice, greed and violence seem able to alter or neutralize the power of God's providence toward the children He loves.

## III I Will Espouse You to Me Forever

This figure of the love and faithfulness of marriage appears frequently in the Scriptures. Here again, only faith and prayer can bring some *realization* of the meaning of this union of man and God. If two human hearts can experience ecstasy in a union of love, what of the union of the human and divine, of man and God?

St. Paul tells us that faith anticipates what God has prepared for those who love Him: things delightful beyond anything eyes have seen, ears have heard, or man's fertile imagination has conceived.[5]

*I will espouse you to me forever:*
*I will espouse you in right and in justice,*
*in love and in mercy....*[6]

*My lover speaks; he says to me,*
*"Arise, my beloved, my beautiful one, and come!*
*"For see, the winter is past....*
*Let me see you,*
*let me hear your voice...."*[7]

1. Ps. 103:13 (responsorial psalm, B)
2. Ps. 103:8-10
3. Is. 49:14-15 (first reading, A)
4. Mt. 6:30 (Gospel, A)
5. Cf. 1 Cor. 2:9
6. Hos. 2:21 (first reading, B)
7. Sg. 2:10-11, 14

## Ninth Sunday of the Year

(B)

*For God, who said, "Let light shine out of darkness," has shone in our hearts, that we in turn might make known the glory of God shining on the face of Christ.*[1]

*Of you my heart speaks...*
*your presence, O Lord, I seek.*
*Hide not your face from me....*[2]

Lord, this is my heart at prayer. It sets out to search for You, at times aware of Your presence; yet desiring that intimate communication that is only possible "face to face."

O God, You have many presences. We find You in some manner in all that touches our lives. We marvel at Your infinity as we look to the starry heavens and wrestle with those numbers designating mass, distance and energy. We see the might of Your outstretched arms when we stand by the sea, so expansive and yet so restless in the confines of the unmeasured shore. Your fingers are behind a snowflake, a wing, a blossom; Your voice in harmonies of birdsong, running waters, music. Your knowledge and wisdom are manifest in the hierarchies, diversities and laws discernible in all man's categories of scientific knowledge. We trace Your footprints in the stages of the evolving earth; sense Your goodness and prodigality in the skyline of a great city, in the fertile acres of wheatland.

O God, Your loving, working, sustaining presence in all about us is marvelous. But not enough! This presence only increases the desire to meet You face to face.

We humans communicate in many ways: by letter, by phone, by gifts, by signs and bodily attitudes. But what a different communication is intimate interchange, face to face, of lover or perfect friend. How much of the soul's deepest movements are passed from face to face: gladness, gratitude, sympathy, longing, love—and hurt, sadness, reproach. O God, to communicate thus with You! We deeply desire it—perhaps foolishly risk it.

If we have a measure of love—even a *desire* to love—we search for the glance of Your eyes. As we pray, You may seem to us a dim figure, a benign but shapeless presence; or even as having Your back turned to us. But we go on praying, in humility and hope, *that we may perceive the glory of God shining on the face of Christ....*

And we hope to see You, in the time You appoint, "face to face."

*He looked around at them with anger....*[3]

Please, Lord Jesus, not that! That was the face You turned toward those who resisted You. But if we do not clearly see Your face, is it perhaps because we have not understood that You wish us first to recognize You in masquerade? You put on faces of many hues and features; masks of comedy and tragedy; the face of tears as well as of smiles. We do not recognize You in our own family; when we pass You on the street; or see You shining shoes or selling newspapers. We don't think of looking for You in a picket line or in jail, on skid row or in a ward of the county hospital. Failing to see Your face in the face of one of these least of Your brothers, we may be all unprepared to see You unmasked, in face-to-face revelation which brings the delight of loving union.

1. 2 Cor. 4:6 (second reading, B)
2. Ps. 27:8
3. Mk. 3:5 (Gospel, B)

## Tenth Sunday of the Year

Read Gn. 3:9-15
Mk. 3:20-35

The readings for this Sunday (B) present two common and serious flaws in our relationships with each other: passing the blame and detraction.

### I Passing the Buck

After Adam had eaten from the tree whose fruit had been forbidden to him, he hid himself, but the Lord called to him. He replied:

> *"...I was afraid, because I was naked, so I hid myself." Then he asked, "Who told you that you were naked? You have eaten, then, from the tree of which I had forbidden you to eat!" The man replied, "The woman whom you put here with me—she gave me fruit from the tree, and so I ate it." The Lord God then asked the woman, "Why did you do such a thing?" The woman answered, "The serpent tricked me into it, so I ate it."*[1]

We are very much sons of Adam. When conscious of sin, we too may feel naked and ashamed, afraid and anxious to hide. This nakedness is the loss of dignity and self-possession because of the loss of grace with which we had been clothed through God's gift. In our shame, partly because of fear, partly because of pride, we clutch at excuses, eager to pass the blame to others. Adam blames "the woman whom you put here with me," as though God Himself was partly responsible for his failure. Eve in turn blames the serpent, the tempter. "The devil made me do it" has become a sort of by-line for a television comedian. Though the expression provides comedy, it also conveys a common attitude of sinful man. He is inclined to blame the devil or anyone or anything else for his failings rather than himself. In the story of Adam, God would seem to admit some measure of mitigation of their sin by His curse upon the serpent; but immediately after He metes out heavy punishment to Eve and Adam because, in spite of temptation, their choosing of evil was still free.

This buck-passing is instinctive, a defense mechanism that causes us, like a punch-drunk boxer, to throw up our guard at the sound of any bell.

Shame and fear at sin must give way to humble admission of guilt and trust in forgiveness and restoration of our dignity.

*Out of the depths I cry to you, O Lord;*
*Lord, hear my voice!*
*Let your ears be attentive*
*to my voice in supplication:*
*...But with you is forgiveness,*
*that you may be revered.*[2]

## II Detracting From Others

Our tendency is to downgrade others as though this automatically raised our own spiritual status. We often put the worst interpretation on their actions; we may impugn their motives when their actions are seemingly good.

Jesus was the victim of pettiness and misjudgment on the part of His relatives and the plain malice of His enemies.

> *...again the crowd assembled, making it impossible for them to get any food whatever. When his family heard of this they came to take charge of him, saying, "He is out of his mind"; while the scribes who arrived from Jerusalem asserted, "He is possessed by Beelzebub," and "He expels demons with the help of the prince of demons."*[3]

## III Relating to Christ

Breaches of charity such as the foregoing are of course primary obstacles to our properly relating to the God of love and to Christ who died for those whom we will not even give a fair break in our judgments.

When we overcome by real love these egocentric tendencies to diminish others and exalt ourselves, the way is open to an intimate relationship with Jesus. When surrounded by a crowd that gathered to hear Him, Jesus was given the message that His mother and relatives wanted to talk to Him. Looking at those about Him, He said,

> *"These are my mother and my brothers. Whoever does the will of God is brother and sister and mother to me."*[4]

Wonderful as was the close relationship of Mary with her Son because of her motherhood, it would have been meaningless without that rapport resulting from her constant attention to the will of God, His Father. On another occasion,

*...a woman from the crowd called out, "Blest is the womb that bore you and the breasts that nursed you!" "Rather," he replied, "blest are they who hear the word of God and keep it."*[5]

Jesus, let others see that I am Your brother, Your sister. Let there be a family resemblance between myself and Your mother and all those others who hear the word of God and keep it.

1. Gn. 3:10-13 (first reading)
2. Ps. 130:1-2, 4 (responsorial psalm)
3. Mk. 3:20-22 (Gospel)
4. Mk. 3:34-35
5. Lk. 11:27-28

Eleventh Sunday of the Year

Read Mk. 4:26-34
Ez. 17:22-24
(B)

## I Hear of the Kingdom of God

Jesus speaks of the kingdom of God in parables, each of them giving some aspect of this kingdom; then the hearer must search for a deeper and more satisfactory knowledge through the desire that faith generates. Like the disciples, we must come in good will, faith, and desire for this kingdom. The indifferent are given enough to pique their curiosity and lead them to search for greater knowledge.

For the disciples,

> *"To you has been given a knowledge of the mysteries of the reign of God, but it has not been given to the others."*[1]

> *...he kept explaining things privately to his disciples.*[2]

There are many who are not ready for a clear revelation of the mystery of the kingdom, who refuse to see and hear, who are afraid of being converted and healed because of the cost,

> *...otherwise they might see with their eyes,*
> *and hear with their ears,*
> *and understand with their hearts,*

*and turn back to me,*
*and I should heal them.*[3]

## II Shelter and Grow in It

The Lord says that the kingdom of God is like a very small seed but grows into a large shrub whose branches provide a shaded resting place for the birds.[4] The kingdom has become the shelter for all that fly, every winged creature, those that can rise above the earth and move with freedom and speed. Earth is their home but they easily rise to heavenly things of faith.

*I, too, will take from the crest of the cedar,*
*from its topmost branches tear off a tender shoot,*
*And plant it on a high and lofty mountain....*
*Birds of every kind shall dwell beneath it,*
*every winged thing in the shade of its boughs.*[5]

The kingdom is a great cedar planted and cared for by God. In another aspect, each individual member who has entered that kingdom wholeheartedly is also a flourishing plant:

*The just man shall flourish like the palm tree,*
*like a cedar of Lebanon shall he grow.*
*They that are planted in the house of the Lord*
*shall flourish in the courts of our God.*[6]

## III In Confidence and Humility

The great tree does not stand on the heights without a measure of danger; nor is the small, struggling tree without hope of a marked development, for

*...I, the Lord,*
*Bring low the high tree,*
*lift high the lowly tree,*
*Wither up the green tree,*
*and make the withered tree bloom.*[7]

Lord Jesus, with St. Paul[8] we also are confident and want to be at home with You. And even though we face a judgment according to all that we have done, we shall have confidence, not so much on our profession of being always intent on pleasing You but upon Your own love and faithfulness:

*It is good to give thanks to the Lord,*
*to sing praise to your name, Most High,*
*To proclaim your kindness at dawn and your faithfulness throughout the night.*[9]

It is this, Lord, that will make us flourish like palm trees in the vigorous span of our lives; and if it pleases You to leave us on earth until old age, Your love and faithfulness will keep us spiritually young, fruitful for Your glory:

*They shall bear fruit even in old age;*
*vigorous and sturdy shall they be,*
*Declaring how just is the Lord,*
*my Rock, in whom there is no wrong.*[10]

1. Mt. 13:11
2. Mk. 4:34 (Gospel, B)
3. Mt. 13:15
4. Cf. Mk. 4:30-32 (Gospel, B)
5. Ez. 17:22-23 (first reading, B)
6. Ps. 92:13-14 (responsorial psalm, B)
7. Ez. 17:24
8. Cf. 2 Cor. 5:6-10 (second reading, B)
9. Ps. 92:2-3 (responsorial psalm, B)
10. Ps. 92:15-16

## Twelfth Sunday of the Year

Read Mk. 4:35-40
(B)

# I Does It Not Matter to You That We Are Going To Drown?[1]

Is Peter's boat going down? And perhaps the Ship of State also? Sometimes we may be inclined to think so. We are tossed about by winds of different opinion, lashed by waves of civil disobedience, racial tension, organized protest; caught in cross currents of conflicting ideas of morals and modes of living. Progress seems uncertain; perhaps even the port is invisible in the fog. Yet we know that Peter's boat will never go down.

*...other boats accompanied him.*

Peter's ship, though, should take the lead, for Christ is in it. She has the navigation charts—sound doctrine and noble ideals. If at times there seems to be little progress, let us reflect on our own performance. We *are* the Church: you, I, the neighbor. It is easy to acknowledge corporate failure, harder to see that our own occasional, perhaps small, personal failures—and even more, habitual indifference—add up to a large failure, a great inertia.

When threatened with chaos, we cry out to the Lord, *Does it not matter to you?* He replies, *Why are you so terrified? Why are you lacking in faith?*

We may well be frightened if we depend on our own efforts with oar and sail, if we forget that Jesus is in the boat with us. At times He seems asleep and oblivious to our fears and danger. He is not angry if we wake Him with our cries for help, our insistent prayers. It is only if our fears overcome our trust, or if our self-reliance overbalances our confidence in Him, that He chides us.

## II Who Can This Be?

We must always come back to the foundation for confidence, equanimity and peace: our faith in Jesus Christ. *...the wind and sea obey him.* This was proof enough for the disciples that Jesus was more than mere man. "Who can this be?" As the first reading (B) tells us, God alone controls the mighty sea:

*And who shut within doors the sea,*
*when it burst forth from the womb;*
*When I made the clouds its garment*
*and thick darkness its swaddling bands?*
*When I set limits for it*
*and fastened the bar of its door,*
*And said: Thus far shall you come but no farther,*
*and here shall your proud waves be stilled!*[2]

In the Gospel for Cycle C it is Jesus who asks the great question, *Who do you say I am?*[3] The reply *we* now give was very difficult for the Jews of His time, and the full answer came to the apostles slowly. Peter takes a big step when he declares that Jesus is the Christ of God, the Messiah. Later, in a letter attributed to him, we have a development of faith which proposes the eternity of Christ and our redemption through His death:

> *Realize that you were delivered from the futile way of life...not by any diminishable sum...but by Christ's blood beyond all price: the blood of a spotless, unblemished lamb chosen before the world's foundation and revealed for your sake in these last days.*[4]

Jesus, You are revealed to us, and by the mercy of the Father we believe in You as Savior and Lord. We trust in You as we make our way through a world which at times seems a sea of stormy, threatening events.

> *They cried to the Lord in their distress;*
> *from their straits he rescued them.*
> *He hushed the storm to a gentle breeze,*
> *and the billows of the sea were stilled;*
> *They rejoiced that they were calmed,*
> *and he brought them to their desired haven.*
> *Let them give thanks to the Lord for his kindness*
> *and his wondrous deeds to the children of men.*[5]

1. Cf. Mk. 4:35-40 (Gospel, B)
2. Jb. 38:8-11
3. Lk. 9:20
4. 1 Pt. 1:18-20
5. Ps. 107:28-31 (responsorial psalm, B)

## Thirteenth Sunday of the Year

Read Lk. 9:51-62
1 Kgs. 19:19-21
(C, A)

### I Service in the Spirit

The idea of vocation is much in evidence in the readings for this Sunday: the call to respond to God's invitation to a special service for Him. This call to live for God, to live in the Spirit, means death to self-indulgence.

> *...you should live in accord with the spirit and you will not yield to the cravings of the flesh. The flesh lusts against the spirit and the spirit against the flesh; the two are directly opposed. This is why you do not do what your will intends.*[1]

If we would give outstanding service to Christ, whether in a religious state or lay, we must "put on Christ." Before we can do this we must strip ourselves of all that serves mere self-indulgence. We are to love men more intensely for the love of Christ. This includes those naturally loved as relatives and close friends, but the expression of this love is always secondary to the demands of the work of Christ, the spreading of the Good News.

*To another he said, "Come after me." The man replied, "Let me bury my father first." Jesus said to him, "Let the dead bury their dead; come away and proclaim the kingdom of God."*[2]

## II Commitment

This work requires a commitment that is both total and permanent. A young man all set to follow Jesus wanted to go home for a proper leave-taking, but Jesus said,

*"Whoever puts his hand to the plow but keeps looking back is unfit for the reign of God."*[3]

We commit ourselves to God out of love. We must be faithful as He Himself is faithful.

*The favors of the Lord I will sing forever;*
*through all generations my mouth shall proclaim your faithfulness.*
*For you have said, "My kindness is established forever";*
*in heaven you have confirmed your faithfulness.*[4]

When Elijah was told to anoint Elisha as his successor and he went to the field where the latter was plowing, and threw his cloak over him in a symbolic transfer of authority and power, Elisha immediately followed him. But he hesitated at the thought of a proper leave-taking of his parents. When Elijah rebuked him, Elisha graphically expressed his complete surrender and change of life: he killed his oxen, cooked them with the wood of his plow, ate a last meal with his men, and then became Elijah's servant. This stripping of self-love and sublimation of natural human love, this total dedication, Christ calls "losing one's life"—but it is only to find a new, more purposeful, more fulfilling and so, more joyous life.

> *Whoever loves father or mother, son or daughter, more than me is not worthy of me. He who will not take up his cross and come after me is not worthy of me. He who seeks only himself brings himself to ruin, whereas he who brings himself to nought for me discovers who he is.*[5]

## III Liberty of God's Sons

Francis of Assisi is one of those who took the Lord's words more literally. Renouncing family, position and wealth, having nothing but the rough peasant's clothes he was wearing, he went happily singing the praises of God, in a carefree brotherhood with those birds of the air and lilies of the field so amply provided for by providence, keenly appreciative of all those taken-for-granted blessings: the sun, the stars, all creatures of earth. He was happy in being as poor, and yet as rich, as his Lord.

> *"The foxes have lairs, the birds of the sky have nests, but the Son of Man has nowhere to lay his head."*[6]

Such total poverty provides great freedom, but of course it is not possible to most men, especially to those with family obligations. But all who wish to serve in a significant way and to enjoy Christ's freedom must heed Paul's directive to forget self and turn in loving service to others.

*My brothers, remember that you have been called to live in freedom—but not a freedom that gives free rein to the flesh. Out of love, place yourselves at one another's service. The whole law has found its fulfillment in this one saying: "You shall love your neighbor as yourself."*[7]

1. Gal. 5:16-17 (second reading, C)
2. Lk. 9:59-60 (Gospel, C)
3. Lk. 9:62
4. Ps. 89:2-3 (responsorial psalm, A)
5. Mt. 10:37-39 (Gospel, A)
6. Lk. 9:58
7. Gal. 5:13-14 (second reading, C)

## Fourteenth Sunday of the Year

Read Ez. 2:2-5
Mk. 6:1-7
(B)

# I The Carpenter

Jesus was in His home town, Nazareth, with His disciples:

> *When the sabbath came he began to teach in the synagogue in a way that kept his large audience amazed.... Is this not the carpenter, the son of Mary...?"*[1]

They knew Him well, this Jesus, the carpenter's son, and Himself a carpenter. They knew His mother, too: kindly, sensitive to others, but essentially a simple homemaker, wife and mother. They knew His cousins and other relatives, all typical people of a little town out of the mainstream of culture and erudition. Jesus "belonged." He was a bit unusual in that He was still unmarried and living with His parents at nearly thirty years of age, but an average village resident, like His parents, quiet, unobtrusive, undistinguished.

But now suddenly He is teaching in the synagogues and on the streets. This is a little too much, the carpenter who has never been a pupil of the rabbis making Himself out a teacher—and with a special insight and authority, a message of "Good News" and a demand for change of heart.

> *"Where did he get all this? What kind of wisdom is he endowed with?... They found him too much for them.*[2]

## II A Prophet

The prophet Ezekiel is sent to a people who are not ready to receive God's message and submit to His loving care (first reading, B). He is told that he is being sent to rebels, men defiant and obstinate. He is to give them God's word even though they were not likely to listen.

The prophets are always sent to speak to those who are rebels before God; but they themselves are usually considered the rebels, because the world to which they speak has commonly accepted attitudes and ways that deviate from the difficult ideals of justice and love upon which God is insisting. Jesus Himself was no doubt a rebel in the eyes of many of His contemporaries, criticizing their practice of religion and moral failures. It was not until He left the quiet life of Nazareth and began His controversial teaching that the people of Palestine knew there was a prophet among them.

## III The Word of God

When we think of how His fellow-townsmen looked upon Jesus, the carpenter, what a gigantic leap we take when we believe in Him as Son of God, see Him as the early Church came to see, and especially as Paul and John knew Him.

*God did not send the Son into the world*
*to condemn the world,*
*but that the world might be saved through*
*him.*[3]

*[God] bestowed on him the name*
*above every other name,*
*So that at Jesus' name*
*every knee must bend...*
*and every tongue proclaim*
*to the glory of God the Father:*
*JESUS CHRIST IS LORD!*[4]

Lord Jesus, You have said that only the Father knows the Son and only the Son knows the Father. But You do wish to be known, to reveal Yourself to those who look for You. This is our earnest prayer, that we may know You; and then we will know the Father also, in the light and power of the Spirit.

Lord, increase our faith!

1. Mk. 6:2-3 (Gospel, B)
2. Mk. 6:2-3
3. Jn. 3:17
4. Phil. 2:9-11

## Fifteenth Sunday of the Year

Read Eph. 1:3-17
Col. 1:15-20
(B)

# I A New Creature

Lost in a crowd of fifty thousand sports fans; jostling anonymous bodies in a jammed subway; watching a parade of thousands of soldiers dressed alike and keeping step; listening to the dire warnings of pessimistic demographers and ecologists—these situations make it difficult to realize the worth of every human person. The full dignity of a man is seen only in faith, as expressed in Ephesians.[1]

> *God chose us in him before the world began...; he...predestined us through Christ Jesus to be his adopted sons.... In him we were chosen; ...in the decree of God, who administers everything....*

Christian dignity cannot be taken away by men or lost through circumstance; it can only be renounced.

We can have delusions about what gives dignity to a person. This nobility can exist, be pre-eminent, in the seemingly ignoble and despised. It does not require the body of a Mr. America or a Miss Universe; nor the face that graces magazine covers. It can be hidden in the painful frame of a paralytic or wasted body of a terminal cancer patient; behind the face entirely ungraced by nature or scarred by accident. It may be covered by the sweaty clothes of a laborer or the inexpensive evening gown. It is not enhanced by all the arts of the vanity table. This nobility may have as its palace a small apartment with crumbling walls and broken plumbing. It is more likely to be present in a crowded bus of working people than on a private yacht cruising pleasant seas. The chosen of God are often those who are nothing in the esteem of men.

## II Vision of Faith

Lord Jesus, give us eyes of faith that penetrate appearances and glimpse the worth and beauty of every person chosen in Christ, every Christian and even potential Christian. Give us the faith that first sees and accepts You, man of Nazareth, poor and laboring, as *the image of the invisible God, the first-born of all creatures*[2]; holds that the eternal God has sent us His Son in order to *bring all things in the heavens and on the earth into one under Christ's headship.* From this vision of You, O Christ, let us pass to discovery, under the most deceptive disguises, of the dignity of every human—chosen, in Christ, *to be holy and blameless,* and *to be full of love, to be his adopted sons...sealed with the Holy Spirit.*

Make us truly to live through love in Your presence. This is possible only because *immeasurably generous is God's favor to us.* It will be possible, Lord, only when we remember that You made peace by Your death on the cross, and that, free as we are and joyful in faith, we walk in the shadow of the cross.

Lord Jesus, for all of our vision of dignity, we are deeply aware of being wounded and wretched, in constant need of being restored in grace and strength to love.

*But I pray to you, O Lord....*
*In your great kindness answer me*
*with your constant help....*
*But I am afflicted and in pain;*
*let your saving help, O God, protect me.*
*I will praise the name of God in song,*
*and I will glorify him with thanksgiving....*[3]

1. Cf. Eph. 1:4-14 (second reading, B)
2. Col. 1:15 (second reading, C)
3. Ps. 69:14, 30-31 (responsorial psalm, C)

Sixteenth Sunday of the Year

Read Mk. 6:30-34
(B, A)

## I Come and Rest a Little

*The apostles returned to Jesus and reported to him all that they had done and what they had taught. He said to them, "Come by yourselves to an out-of-the-way place and rest a little." People were coming and going in great numbers, making it impossible for them to so much as eat.*[1]

The ever-accelerating change of our world today catches up each of us in its current, where we struggle to keep upright, our head above water. We needlessly increase our activity by our drive to have more and better *things* in our lives, as reflected in today's tremendous do-it-yourself market. We seem never so satisfied with our present level of possessions or comfort that we can relax and properly enjoy what we have or take up those activities that improve the mind and strengthen the spirit.

More reasonable and justified is the tension and drive of those who feel the absolute urgency of working for a just social order and God's kingdom of universal love. Many religious, priests and lay apostles, find themselves in the situation of those first twelve men who gave themselves to Christ's work: "there were so many coming and going that the apostles had no time even to eat."

The apostolic worker of this space age is certainly more in need of withdrawal for rejuvenation of spirit than men of Christ's footpath and camel-trail days. He must have times for quiet appraisal of himself and his work, for renewing inspiration and rekindling enthusiasm, for more intense and prolonged prayer. In this prayer he learns and puts on Christ; only then can he show Him and give Him to others.

Prayer is not specifically mentioned here, but rather rest and withdrawal. Yet can we doubt that it was an invitation to a prayerful rest, a retreat, when we consider Jesus' own frequent retirement for prayer?

> *When he had sent them away, he went up on the mountain by himself to pray, remaining there alone as evening drew on.*[2]
>
> *Rising early the next morning, he went off to a lonely place in the desert; there he was absorbed in prayer.*[3]
>
> *Then he went out to the mountain to pray, spending the night in communion with God.*[4]

## II But I Can't Pray

This is a common complaint of the average busy man—as well as the active apostolic worker—who finds it very difficult to "let go," to clear his mind of the numerous details and needs of his work, and to quiet his soul for receptivity to the Holy Spirit. It is at least a comfort to recall that we need only to strive for this tranquillity and openness, and not to be suddenly gifted with marvelous insights and an eloquence pouring out praise and petition that heaven cannot possibly resist.

*The Spirit too helps us in our weakness, for we do not know how to pray as we ought; but the Spirit himself makes intercession for us with groanings that cannot be expressed in speech. He who searches hearts knows what the Spirit means....*[5]

This is the important part of our prayer: what we have in our hearts. We lay open to the Spirit, even without words, our deepest desires.

God delights to fill the emptiness we humbly acknowledge, to *give good things to anyone who asks him!*[6]

*Lord, teach us to pray!*[7]

1. Mk. 6:30-31 (Gospel, B)
2. Mt. 14:23-24
3. Mk. 1:35
4. Lk. 6:12
5. Rom. 8:26-27 (second reading, A)
6. Mt. 7:11
7. Lk. 11:1

# Seventeenth Sunday of the Year

Read Lk. 11:1-13
(C)

This liturgy gives us lessons on the manner in which we should ask for things in prayer.

## I Persistence

In the first reading (Cycle C) we have Abraham's classic bargaining with the Lord. He is bold and yet humble before the Lord, who is patient to the end. The Lord God is presented in a very human manner, going down to Sodom to check personally on the guilt of the inhabitants; ready then to bargain with Abraham about the punishment to be imposed; seemingly anxious to hear some good reason to grant the requested mercy. Abraham gains the concession that Sodom will not be destroyed if there are found fifty just men in it—then forty-five, forty, and finally,

> *"What if there are at least ten there?" "For the sake of those ten," he replied, "I will not destroy it."*[1]

Abraham failed to find his ten. We see here God's magnanimous mercy and man's failure to fulfill even a minimum condition.

In the Gospel story (C) of the man who goes to his friend in the middle of the night to borrow food and is finally admitted and given it, we are encouraged to be persistent to the point of seeming obnoxious.[2] A similar story is about a certain judge *who respected neither God nor man,* but who finally grants a widow's petition for justice because *this widow is wearing me out.* This story is introduced as a *parable on the necessity of praying always and not losing heart.*[3]

## II Confidence

> *"For whoever asks, receives; whoever seeks, finds; whoever knocks, is admitted.*[4]

It is difficult for us to accept these words at face value. We would say from experience that we have not always received what we asked, found what we searched for in prayer, or had the door of God's presence opened to us.

The very insistence in the Scriptures on *perseverance* in prayer precludes always receiving *immediately* what we ask for. And perhaps we are promised only that our Father in heaven hears us, not that He will always give exactly what we ask. As would an earthly father, He gives what He knows would be for our best interests. He is a Father who knows not only our character and present needs but our future.

> *What father among you will give his son a snake if he asks for a fish, or hand him a scorpion if he asks for an egg? If you, with all your sins, know how to give your children good things, how much more will the heavenly Father give the Holy Spirit to those who ask him.*[5]

In Matthew the parallel passage reads: *how much more will your heavenly Father give good things to anyone who asks him.* But here in Luke's account we have a clue to the careful and loving giving of the heavenly Father to His children: He may withhold some lesser gift but give us the Holy Spirit, the very greatest of gifts.

From other Scripture passages we may infer that we have often received, though perhaps unaware of it, more or better than we asked:

> The man forgiven the debt of 10,000 talents had asked only for more time to repay, but the whole debt was canceled.
>
> The paralyzed man let down through the roof in front of Christ, in addition to being cured, was forgiven all his sins.
>
> The returning prodigal, hoping for a chance to make up for his disgraceful conduct by working as a servant, was immediately reinstated as a loved son.
>
> Solomon's request for wisdom to rule his people so pleased the Lord that he was promised greater wisdom than any before him had possessed, and in addition, riches and glory.
>
> *The Lord is just in all his ways*
> *and holy in all his works.*
> *The Lord is near to all who call upon him,*
> *to all who call upon him in truth.*[6]

1. Cf. Gn. 18:20-32
2. Cf. Lk. 11:5-8
3. Cf. Lk. 18:1-5
4. Lk. 11:10
5. Lk. 11:11-13
6. Ps. 145:17-18 (responsorial psalm, B)

## On Praying for Little Things

When a *world* calls for meet reparation,
when hatred of nation for nation
the very earth's axis must shake—
and *your* prayer's so personal, prosaic,

When heaven's not hearing your sigh
for the din of *humanity's* cry,
or it seems you seek rose in December,
then Cana and Mary remember:

Jesus' world-winning mission was near
but the time and place were not here.
He soon would dispense life divine;
the need here was only for wine.

Not by bread, not by wine, does man live.
His work is to heal, to forgive,
be Consoler and Teacher and Priest;
dare she ask Him to save a groom's feast?

But Mother knew Son, heart and mind.
(Two lives thirty years intertwined.)
And this key to His heart she gives you:
"Whatever he says to you, do."

## Eighteenth Sunday of the Year

Read Eccl. 1:2; 2:21-23
Lk. 12:13-21
(C)

### I Vanity! Emptiness! Fool!

These are words of mockery and bitterness to one whose spirit is weary and disillusioned after long and laborious pursuit of some seeming good. Suddenly the stored harvest is moldy and worm-infested; the gold is tarnished and counterfeit; the pleasures and excitement have turned to boredom and disgust; security, to uncertainty and fear.

> *"A man may be wealthy, but his possessions do not guarantee him life."*[1]

In modern society there is much of insecurity, even among the peoples of the richer nations. A large proportion of the population is without a significant and real ownership, and the majority of those who do own a little are still totally dependent on keeping a steady job in an economy always subject to fluctuation and depression. Jesus does not, of course, condemn a reasonable concern; He does reprove those who become overly concerned and unbalanced in their sense of values.

When one who has seldom or never suffered from real want urges upon the poor a trust in God's

Providence, he may well invite resentment and anger. Nevertheless, it is the *Lord's* invitation, given to the poor who were His daily company, and it is still going out to the poor of today.

> *"I warn you, then: do not worry about your livelihood, what you are to eat or drink or use for clothing.... Look at the birds in the sky. They do not sow or reap.... If God can clothe in such splendor the grass of the field...will he not provide much more for you, O weak in faith!"*[2]

## II To Whom Will This Piled-up Wealth Go?

God reserves the harsh word "Fool!" for the man who becomes wholly occupied with making money, with securing every luxury and pleasure, depending on his own work and cleverness for a complete security.

> *"There was a rich man who had a good harvest. 'What shall I do?' he asked himself. 'I have no place to store my harvest.... I will pull down my grain bins and build larger ones.... Then I will say to myself: ...Relax! Eat heartily, drink well. Enjoy yourself.' But God said to him, 'You fool! This very night your life shall be required of you. To whom will all this piled-up wealth of yours go?'"*[3]

O Lord Jesus, when I stand stripped of my physical powers and my possessions, at the door of death, let me not be tormented, I beg You, by the echo of these words in my failing ears: *vanity!*—all

I have acquired beyond my needs and the purpose of charity; *emptiness!*—the condition of my heart if I cling to possessions; *fool!*—my personal appraisal if I have not made myself "rich in the sight of God."

## III You Who Have No Money, Come!

The desire for money, which makes possible luxuries, pleasures and power, becomes a dominating force in the lives of many.

Opposed to this desire is a hunger and thirst that distinguishes the wise man from the fool, the truly rich from the poor man with many possessions. Those who are blessed with the poverty of the beatitudes, a simple humility and detachment, are invited to God's table.

*All you who are thirsty,*
*come to the water!*
*You who have no money,*
*come, receive grain and eat;*
*Come, without paying and without cost,*
*drink wine and milk!*
*Why spend your money for what is not bread;*
*your wages for what fails to satisfy?*
*Heed me, and you shall eat well,*
*you shall delight in rich fare.*
*Come to me heedfully,*
*listen, that you may have life.*[4]

Is he rich who holds the deed
to many things—but less than need?
Or he who by a heavenly art
contrives with few to fill his heart?

1. Lk. 12:15 (Gospel, C)
2. Mt. 6:25-30
3. Lk. 12:16-20
4. Is. 55:1-3 (first reading, A)

Nineteenth Sunday of the Year

Read 1 Kgs. 19:4-16
Jn. 6:41-51
(B)

## I I've Had It!

> *[Elijah] went a day's journey into the desert, until he came to a broom tree and sat beneath it. He prayed for death: "This is enough, O Lord! Take my life, for I am no better than my fathers."*[1]

There may have been occasions when we felt as depressed and discouraged as Elijah when he had "had enough," and was ready even to quit this life. We can be brought very low by a sense of failure, loneliness, rejection, or by persistent personal difficulties.

Elijah's discouragement arose from his failure as a prophet to bring his people to a grateful and loving relationship with the God who had so favored them. This was at least a noble reason for depression, but God would not allow him to give up. Discouragement can lead to that species of self-indulgence which abandons all effort.

St. Paul also felt the anguish, if not the discouragement, of Elijah because of his own deep insight into the blessings of Christ which were being rejected by the people of God's choice, his brothers. He is driven by his sorrow to words that seem irrational:

> *...I do not lie.... There is great grief and constant pain in my heart. Indeed, I could even wish to be separated from Christ for the sake of my brothers....*[2]

These are the amazing words of the man who had also said that Christ was his very life,[3] that he lived with the life of Christ,[4] that knowing Christ, having Christ, made him see everything else as unnecessary and worthless.[5]

O God, that our own discouragement and sorrow might arise only from zeal for Your honor and understanding concern for others, not from preoccupation with selfish interests.

## II Right on!

In a continuation of the story of Elijah from the First Book of Kings we find the Lord urging him on to His work, in spite of mortal danger.

> *"Elijah, why are you here?" He replied, "I have been most zealous for the Lord, the God of hosts. But the Israelites have forsaken your covenant, torn down your altars, and put your prophets to the sword. I alone am left, and they seek to take my life." "Go, take the road back,..." the Lord said....*[6]

Elijah was revived in spirit and enabled to continue in the Lord's work by food provided by an angel. He walked forty days and forty nights, until he reached the "Mountain of God." Moses had spent forty days on this mountain in the presence of God. Here Elijah was to find God, too, and be confirmed in the work given him. We have the true bread of life, strengthening us to walk to the mountain where we have our own vision of God, through Christ. *Whoever has seen me has seen the Father.*[7]

## III To the Vision of God

Elijah's walk of forty days and forty nights is an echo of the Hebrew's forty years of wandering in the desert, when they were sustained by manna "from heaven." Forty days was the length of Jesus' life on earth in His glorified body before He returned to the eternal life He shared with His Father in heaven. Forty years represent roughly a generation, the measure of a life, for it is approximately the span of the active adult life. The vision of God in life everlasting follows our earthly sojourn because Jesus has given His own *flesh, for the life of the world.*[8]

In his earthly life the "flesh" in a physical sense was given very little consideration, and in the end very painfully sacrificed. The Christian must view at least with suspicion the cult of the body beautiful, and pleasures of sense so constantly and attractively urged upon us today. Care of the body and sensual enjoyment are not evil in themselves; they become so when they so dominate our thoughts and desires as to endanger the life which Jesus offers and which is forever.

There is a beauty that comes from an interior goodness and peace of heart, and it can be seen on the faces of young and old, whether physically beautiful or not.

*Look to him that you may be radiant with joy,*
*and your faces may not blush with shame.*[9]

1. 1 Kgs. 19:4 (first reading, B)
2. Rom. 9:1-3 (second reading, A)
3. Cf. Phil. 1:21
4. Cf. Gal. 2:20-21
5. Cf. Phil. 3:8
6. 1 Kgs. 19:13-15
7. Jn. 14:9
8. Jn. 6:51 (Gospel, B)
9. Ps. 34:6 (responsorial psalm, B)

## Twentieth Sunday of the Year

Read Jn. 6:51-58
Eph. 5:15-20
(B)

# I Hard To Endure

*"I myself am the living bread*
*come down from heaven.*
*If anyone eats this bread*
*he shall live forever;*
*the bread I will give*
*is my flesh, for the life of the world."*[1]

Jesus knew these words would be an obstacle for His hearers, but He does not withdraw them. Rather He repeats and fortifies them. Unless they eat and drink of this spiritual food, His very flesh and blood, they will not have in them the life He came to give.

> *...many of his disciples remarked, "This sort of talk is hard to endure! How can anyone take it seriously?"*[2]

This was most difficult for the Jews to accept. And indeed if these words were proposed today to anyone who had no previous knowledge of Christian teaching, he might understandably be repulsed by the seeming cannibalistic cult. This mystery is one which is still difficult for those who are attracted to Christ, and divides those who call themselves Christians.

*Do you think I have come to establish peace on the earth? I assure you, the contrary is true; I have come for division.*[3]

Lord, You also said that You *do* give peace to Your followers. We will not leave You, but follow with a faith that accepts the perplexing words, leaping over the objections raised by refinements of language, sensitivity of culture, antipathy of human reason. We believe just because You said it.

## 11 Wisdom's Table

In humble trust we come to the table which divine wisdom has spread for us. If we have hesitated in our faith, or even foolishly neglected this bread of life, we are invited to return.

*Wisdom has built her house....*
*"Let whoever is simple turn in here;*
*to him who lacks understanding, I say,*
*Come, eat of my food,*
*and drink of the wine I have mixed!*
*Forsake foolishness that you may live....*[4]

*Come, children, hear me....*
*Which of you desires life,*
*and takes delight in prosperous days?*[5]

*...the man who feeds on this bread shall live forever.*[6]

We have already begun to live the eternal life, life of a community united in Christ. We should show now a good measure of that joy which we expect to be eternal.

*...addressing one another in psalms and hymns and inspired songs. Sing praise to the Lord with all your hearts. Give thanks to God the Father always and for everything in the name of our Lord Jesus Christ.*[7]

We thank You, Father in heaven, for calling us to the table Wisdom has set, the table which supports the life of the spirit. Folly too has invited us to her table and at times we were foolish enough to try her fare. But what appealed so strongly to the eye and stimulated our appetites was a sweet fluff, at best without solid nourishment for life eternal, and at worst a poison. We are grateful for Your invitation, and pray that we—and all of hungering humanity—may come to

"Taste and see the goodness of the Lord."[8]

1. Jn. 6:51 (Gospel, B)
2. Jn. 6:60
3. Lk. 12:51 (Gospel, C)
4. Prv. 9:1, 4-6 (first reading, B)
5. Ps. 34:12-13 (responsorial psalm, B)
6. Jn. 6:58
7. Eph. 5:19-20 (second reading, B)
8. Responsorial antiphon, B

## Twenty-first Sunday of the Year

Read Eph. 5:21-32
Jn. 6:59-69
Mt. 16:13-20
(B)

### I Choosing the Lord

In today's Mass we are reminded that each of us must make a deliberate life-orientation, a free choice to serve the Lord. Most of us were baptized as infants. We were chosen by God, but our own response, by proxy then, needs to be ratified, not by one final act, but by a deliberate development of a basic attitude toward God and toward Christ. It is an habitual "Yes" to God's will as it unfolds for us.

We are not much different, though, from the Old Covenant people, who needed constant exhortation to return to God's way which they so readily abandoned:

> *Joshua gathered together all the tribes of Israel.... "If it does not please you to serve the Lord, decide today whom you will serve.... As for me and my household, we will serve the Lord."*[1]

Aware of our infidelities, we should humbly reaffirm our commitment, as did Joshua's audience:

*"Far be it from us to forsake the Lord for the service of other gods."*[2]

In the Gospel (B) we see the followers of Christ given the choice of breaking or continuing with Him in the face of His difficult demands of faith, His strange, repugnant words about eating His flesh.

## II His Church: Mystery

Having committed ourselves to God, we are part of the one Body of Christ. In this union with Christ, risen from death, we are made to live eternally. Whatever our particular "vocation," or the ways and circumstances of our lives, our hope is the same. St. Paul compares a most common way of Christian life, marriage, to the union of Christ and the Church[3]; and Vatican II takes up this theme:

> Christ loves the Church as His bride. For her part, the Church is subject to her Head. "For in him dwells all the fullness of the Godhead bodily" (Col. 2:9). He fills the Church, which is His body and His fullness, with His divine gifts so that she may grow and reach all the fullness of God.[4]

## III And Structure

The same Vatican II document presents two aspects of the Church: the spiritual entity that is the body of believers living in union with Christ and by His life; and the visible, hierarchical structure:

> Christ, the one Mediator, established and ceaselessly sustains here on earth His holy Church, the community of faith, hope, and

> charity as a visible structure. Through her He communicates truth and grace to all. But the society furnished with hierarchical agencies and the Mystical Body of Christ are not to be considered as two realities, nor are the visible assembly and the spiritual community, nor the earthly Church and the Church enriched with heavenly things. Rather they form one interlocked reality which is comprised of a divine and a human element.[5]

In the Gospel we see Peter taking the lead in expression of the faith of the steadfast believers:

> *"You have the words of eternal life. We have come to believe; we are convinced that you are God's holy one."*[6]

In Matthew's Gospel Peter's unique leadership is more strikingly presented. Jesus asks the disciples about what is being said of Himself, then asks them their own opinion. When Peter speaks up to confess Jesus is the Christ, he is declared blessed, and given leadership in the Church.

> *"...you are 'Rock,' and on this rock I will build my church.... I will entrust to you the keys of the kingdom of heaven."*[7]

We may be grateful for the Council's efforts to explain collegiality and to develop its implications. We need to support Pope and bishops, as well as priests and the whole people of God, as they struggle painfully with the many problems encountered in the practical application of co-responsibility in the Church. We may be exasperated with the slowness of the process, or cautious and fearful of the conflict it engenders. In either case we owe it to those burdened with authority to help them with our prayers and cooperation.

*The Lord is exalted, yet the lowly he sees,*
*and the proud he knows from afar,*
*...your kindness, O Lord, endures forever;*
*forsake not the works of your hands.*[8]

1. Jos. 24:1, 15 (first reading, B)
2. Jos. 24:16
3. Cf. Eph. 5:32 (second reading, B)
4. Vatican II, The Church, 7, paragraph 9
5. Vatican II, The Church, 8, paragraph 1
6. Jn. 6:68-69
7. Mt. 16:18-19 (Gospel, A)
8. Ps. 138:6, 8 (responsorial psalm, A)

## Twenty-second Sunday of the Year

Read Dt. 4:1-2, 6-8
Mk. 7:1-8, 14-23
(B)

# I A Perfect Law

Moses was speaking to his people:

> *"Now, Israel, hear the statutes and decrees which I am teaching you.... Observe them carefully, for thus will you give evidence of your wisdom and intelligence to the nations, who will hear of all these statutes and say, 'This great nation is truly a wise and intelligent people.'"*[1]

Through Moses God gave to Israel an exalted, ennobling law, the observance of which would set this people apart from other nations by their wisdom and moral stature. But their history seems like one prolonged struggle between them and the prophets God sent to remind them of the law and to exhort them to keep it.

In the revelation of Jesus Christ the Law has been perfected and completed, Jesus found it necessary to condemn many of those who most ostentatiously professed the keeping of the Law of the Lord.

> *I tell you, unless your holiness surpasses that of the scribes and Pharisees you shall not enter the kingdom of God.*[2]

This is the common religious tragedy, the gap between our profession and our performance. Without a habit of prayerful reflection on ourselves, a discernment made possible by the Holy Spirit, we are ever in danger of self-deception, of distortion of values, of insidious self-justification. We could find ourselves among those of whom Christ says,

> *This people pays me lip service,*
> *but their heart is far from me.*[3]

> *You pay tithes on mint and herbs and seeds while neglecting the weightier matters of the law, justice and mercy and good faith.... You strain out the gnat and swallow the camel!*[4]

## II A Perfect Heart

Jesus enumerates the great evils that may come from men's hearts: sensuality, fornication, adultery; envy, greed; deceit, arrogance, malice, murder. These are the fruits of man's corrupted heart unaided by grace. But Paul indicates the remedy:

> *Since we live by the spirit, let us follow the spirit's lead.*
> *...the fruit of the spirit is love, joy, peace, patient endurance, kindness, generosity, faith, mildness and chastity.*[5]

"Lip service"; holding "human doctrines"; "worthless worship"—because "their hearts are far from me." It is the *heart* that must be given. Deep within our hearts lie our true desires and intentions. Without love no worship or offering is acceptable.

Much more than the people of Moses' time do we say, *What great nation is there that has gods so close to it as the Lord, our God, is to us...?* We have the Son of God among us, His words, His presence in the liturgy and sacraments. We are offered the indwelling of the Holy Spirit. But God awaits the free response of the heart, a heart single-minded and faithful.

*Teach me, O Lord, your way*
*that I may walk in your truth;*
*direct my heart that it may fear your name.*[6]

Yes, Lord God, teach me how to walk Your way. I am so inclined to expect *You* to walk *mine*, to be at my side. I am often asking *You* to be my companion in a way *I* choose, to conform to *my* plans, rather than conforming myself to Yours. And this is the heart of the problem of sin in the Christian soul, the source of all disorders.

Lord, my God, it is not given us on this contentious earth always to know when we are walking Your way, but grant me the single-minded purpose to search out Your way, the single-hearted determination to be faithful. Implant in me that basis of wisdom, "fear of the Lord," reverence for Your sovereign will and unalterable purpose in our world, that my way may be in harmony with all creation and with You, the Creator. Make me strive especially for harmony where it is most lacking, in the peak of Your creation, among men—men whose hearts should conform to the heart of Your Son, who must work with Him to restore the broken unity through justice, love and peace.

1. Dt. 4:1, 6 (first reading, B)
2. Mt. 5:20
3. Mk. 7:6 (Gospel, B)
4. Mt. 23:23-24
5. Gal. 5:25; 22
6. Ps. 86:11

## Twenty-third Sunday of the Year

Read Ez. 33:7-9
Mt. 18:15-20
Rom. 13:8-10
(A, C)

# I Putting Him Straight

It is difficult to know when we ought to correct another and sometimes even more difficult to know how to do it in order to win and not offend him. The prophet Ezekiel is threatened with dire punishment if he does not correct a wicked man according to the Lord's direction.

> *...when you hear me say anything, you shall warn them for me. If I tell the wicked man that he shall surely die, and you do not speak out to dissuade the wicked man from his way, he [the wicked man] shall die for his guilt, but I will hold you responsible for his death.*[1]

Here there is no doubt of the need to correct, but Ezekiel is a prophet who receives unmistakable directions from the Lord. Bishops also, as shepherds and teachers appointed by God, are required to warn and correct. Priests, as sharers in the bishops' work, have a duty at times to do this. Parents have the obvious duty to correct their children, especially in their early years. The duty of an ordinary person to correct his peer is not so clear. But it appears from the words of Jesus that all on occasion may have the duty to correct another for a serious fault, especially if it threatens the good of the community, of the Church. When there is serious threat to the unity in love of the community, it may protect itself from the obstinate evildoer even by rejecting him.

> *If he ignores even the church, then treat him as you would a Gentile or a tax collector.*[2]

## II With Benevolence

> *If he listens to you, you have won your brother over.*[3]

This is the only motive that justifies our attempt to correct another: to win him back to the way of love for God and for others. The only attitude that can succeed is that of *benevolence*, the true desire for the good of the one to be corrected and of the community. There must be no trace of vindictiveness, ill-feeling, superiority or self-justification. If we find any of this in our hearts, the attempt to correct would only aggravate the situation.

We may well be cautious about correcting another. We are at best poor judges, conditioned by our particular education and experience, swayed by appearances and deep-seated, often unrecognized prejudices, unsure in our knowledge of the good and true.

> *...who can conceive what the Lord intends?*
> *For the deliberations of mortals are timid,*
> *and unsure are our plans.*
> *For the corruptible body burdens the soul*
> *and the earthen shelter weighs down the mind that has many concerns.*

*And scarce do we guess the things on earth,*
*and what is within our grasp we find with difficulty;*
*but when things are in heaven, who can search them out?*
*Or who ever knew your counsel, except you had given Wisdom*
*and sent your holy spirit from on high?*[4]

Lord, grant us this Holy Spirit of Wisdom from above. Give us the love without which we take great risk in correcting another even when we have the duty to do so. Lord, with this love we can relate to others with the confidence of Paul, who says love is the answer to every one of the commandments.[5]

Heart of Jesus, fire our hearts with Your love!

1. Ez. 33:7-8 (first reading, A)
2. Mt. 18:17 (Gospel, A)
3. Mt. 18:15
4. Wis. 9:13-17 (first reading, C)
5. Cf. Rom. 13:10 (second reading, A)

## Twenty-fourth Sunday of the Year

Read 1 Tm. 1:12-17
Mt. 18:21-35
(C, A)

### I I Am the Greatest of Sinners

Many of the saints were able sincerely to believe this of themselves. In their intimacy with God in prayer they had gained insight into God's goodness, the magnitude of His gifts to them, and His patient love. They saw clearly their own imperfect, inconstant response because of human weakness and tendency to evil. Without temptation to feelings of superiority, they acknowledged they had received many and special graces. They realized also the possibility of *great difference* in the measure of God's gifts to individuals and the consequent difference in the debt of gratitude and the malice of individual sins.

Looking at St. Paul's life, we may not see how he can call himself the greatest of sinners:

> *I was once a blasphemer, a persecutor, a man filled with arrogance; but because I did not know what I was doing in my unbelief, I have been treated mercifully....*[1]

He does not excuse himself, however, but takes responsibility for the persecution and punishment he had inflicted on the Christian converts even though his actions sprang from his religious enthusiasm for Judaism. He had approved the murder of Stephen, but this too was motivated by zeal and justified by the prescriptions of the Law as he saw them. The saints do not seek self-justification, but have a deep sense of personal failings, and of the chasm between God's goodness and wisdom and their own meanness and fallibility.

We are fortunate if we have this saintly characteristic of a deep sense of sinfulness together with a joyful gratitude for the gift of our election to the new life of grace.

## II But He Chose Me

Every baptized Christian is individually chosen to faith and through faith to a new life. Should we be proud? Why were *we* chosen? Paul gives the reason for God's choice of *him:* the hope and encouragement of other sinners.

> *...Christ Jesus came into the world to save sinners. Of these I myself am the worst. But on that very account I was dealt with mercifully, so that in me, as an extreme case, Jesus Christ might display all his patience, and that I might become an example to those who would later have faith in him and gain everlasting life.*[2]

God's mercy to us must make us merciful to others. We have the parable of the man who was relieved of a great debt, ten thousand talents, but then refused to cancel a small sum owed him by a fellow servant. He was recalled by the master and punished for failing to show mercy in a small matter when he had been forgiven very much.[3] The first reading (A) reinforces the Gospel:

*Forgive your neighbor's injustice;*
*then when you pray, your own sins will be forgiven.*
*Should a man nourish anger against his fellows*
*and expect healing from the Lord?*[4]

God's gifts to us require that we be open-handed to others:

*If a brother or sister has nothing to wear and no food for the day, and you say to them, "Good-bye and good luck! Keep warm and well fed," but do not meet their bodily needs, what good is that?*[5]

Heavenly Father, You have forgiven us so much; teach us to forgive each other. Lord Jesus, You have proved such great love for us; help us to understand effectively how we also ought to love one another.

1. 1 Tm. 1:13 (second reading, C)
2. 1 Tm. 1:15-16
3. Cf. Mt. 18:21 ff.
4. Sir. 28:2-3
5. Jas. 2:15-16 (second reading, B)

## Twenty-fifth Sunday of the Year

Read Mk. 9:30-37
Wis. 2:12, 17-20
(B)

### I Opportunity for Advancement?

There is unique opportunity for advancement in the community of Christ, in His Church. To become Number 1, to reach the top, is possible to anyone. It involves no special talents or training, no back-breaking schedule or unreasonable sacrifices, and certainly no nerve-racking competition. Though not exactly *easy* to attain, the top spot is open to any one of us.

> *"If anyone wishes to rank first, he must remain the last one of all and the servant of all."*[1]

Like the disciples of Jesus, we find it difficult to understand and accept the way He points out as the means for advancement and distinction.

> *They returned to Capernaum and Jesus, once inside the house, began to ask them, "What were you discussing on the way home?" At this they fell silent, for on the way they had been arguing about who was the most important.*[2]

> *Many who are first shall come last, and the last shall come first.*[3]

Jesus, may I learn that the signs and directives I see in this world of mine are not always to be trusted; that even the simple directions "up" and "down" may be reversed. *"Whoever humbles himself shall be exalted."*[4] But let me humble myself not so much in the hope of being exalted as in the desire to follow Your example of service to all.

## II Rewarding Work?

If the disciples did not understand that to become last and least was to be first in the kingdom of God, they could hardly understand that the way to life was death.

> *"The Son of Man is going to be delivered into the hands of men who will put him to death; three days after his death he will rise." ...they failed to understand his words....*[5]

Nor were they ready now to understand that to teach the way to happiness, to offer others the Good News, was to receive for reward hatred and persecution from some men. The reward for following—and presenting to others—the humble and peaceable Christ is not always peace, at least external peace.

> *It was the wicked who*
> *...said among themselves...*
> *"Let us beset the just one, because he is obnoxious to us;*
> *he sets himself against our doings,*
> *Reproaches us for transgressions of the law...."*[6]
>
> *For haughty men have risen up against me...*
> *they set not God before their eyes.*[7]

## III Baby Sitting!

This seems to be a job of first importance in the Lord's community.

> *Then he took a little child, stood him in their midst, and putting his arms around him, said to them, "Whoever welcomes a child such as this for my sake welcomes me."*[8]

Most pleasing to Christ, then, is caring for children, leading the young to Him. Teachers, counselors and parents are very important people among the laborers for the Lord.

Those who are like children, the simple, dependent and trustful, are the most likely candidates for the kingdom of God.

> *...it is to just such as these that the kingdom of God belongs.*[9]

Loving children is a very Christ-like characteristic:

> *Then he embraced them and blessed them, placing his hands on them.*[10]

1. Mk. 9:35 (Gospel, B)
2. Mk. 9:33-34
3. Mt. 19:30
4. Mt. 23:12
5. Mk. 9:31-32
6. Wis. 1:16–2:1; 2:12 (first reading, B)
7. Ps. 54:5 (responsorial psalm, B)
8. Mk. 9:36-37
9. Mk. 10:14
10. Mk. 10:16

## Twenty-sixth Sunday of the Year

Read Nm. 11:25-29
Phil. 2:1-5
(B, A)

# I The Spirit for All

In the first reading (B) we are told that the Spirit which was upon Moses, the leader of the people, was given by the Lord also to seventy elders who were with him. The people acknowledged this; but when the Spirit was also given to two other men who had not been with Moses at the time, the people were jealously protective of the position Moses held among them and resented this seemingly gratuitous gift of the Spirit in independence of their leader.

> *...when a young man quickly told Moses, "Eldad and Medad are prophesying in the camp," Joshua, son of Nun, who from his youth had been Moses' aide, said, "Moses, my lord, stop them." But Moses answered him, "Are you jealous for my sake? Would that all the people of the Lord were prophets! Would that the Lord might bestow his spirit on them all!"*[1]

We have a similar incident in the Gospel, where the disciples are jealous for their Master's power—and perhaps their own sharing in it. John came to

Jesus to report that they had tried to stop an "outsider" from driving out devils in His name. But Jesus replied:

> *"Do not try to stop him. No man who performs a miracle using my name can at the same time speak ill of me. Anyone who is not against us is with us."*[2]

## II Without Envy or Competition

In the above passages there is a corrective for the attitudes some of us may have.

We may wrongly think that since the Roman Catholic Church alone has the full truth, there can be no significant truth or good in other religions.

We may be so impressed with the prime necessity of intellectual convictions and so suspicious of emotional expression that we condemn offhand anyone who makes much of the affective element of religion.

It seems that the Holy Spirit is at work today in a wide spectrum of activities. There is no doubt that lay persons, all the People of God, are being called by the Spirit to a greater sharing of work with the successors of the apostles. In spite of its many tensions and a measure of risk, this call to a community of love and full cooperation in service can renew the face of the earth.

St. Paul warns of three hindrances to our working together in the power of the Holy Spirit: conceit, rivalry, self-assertion.

> *Never act out of rivalry or conceit; rather, let all parties think humbly of others as superior to themselves, each of you looking to others'*

*interests rather than his own. Your attitude must be that of Christ.*[3]

Lord, help me overcome my pre-judgments, my conceited self-confidence and my distrust of others. Make the spirit of competition and narrow self-interest give way to the spirit of unity and love. I beg for deliverance from these sins even though I may not clearly see them within my soul, for

*...who can detect failings?*
*Cleanse me of my unknown faults!*[4]

1. Nm. 11:27-29
2. Mk. 9:39-40 (Gospel, B)
3. Phil. 2:3-5 (second reading, A)
4. Ps. 19:13 (responsorial psalm, B)

## Twenty-seventh Sunday of the Year

Read Is. 5:1-7
(A)

# I Unfruitful Vines

The agricultural images in Scripture may be less meaningful to the urban dweller than to the suburbanite who has some contact with growing things. They were very familiar to the people to whom the prophets spoke and the Lord after them. In the Old Testament, *the vineyard of the Lord of hosts is the house of Israel* (responsorial psalm, A). These people of the Lord are a vineyard cared for lovingly—cultivated, pruned, protected—yet so frequently disappointing in the fruit produced.

> *...he looked for the crop of grapes.*
> *but what it yielded was wild grapes.*[1]

All through their history there is this contest between the chosen people and their God, the Lord complaining of His vineyard which does not yield its expected fruit, and the keepers of the vineyard, the prophets and holy men, averting destruction by their pleas for mercy and another chance.

The Lord says:

> *...judge between me and my vineyard:*
> *What more was there to do for my vineyard*
> *that I had not done?...*

*Now I will let you know*
*what I mean to do to my vineyard:*
*Take away its hedge, give it to grazing,*
*break through its wall, let it be trampled!*
*Yes, I will make it a ruin:*
*it shall not be pruned or hoed,*
*but overgrown with thorns and briars;*
*I will command the clouds*
*not to send rain upon it.*[2]

In reply those keepers of the vineyard who truly love it dare to complain to the Lord, trusting His love and patience:

*A vine from Egypt you transplanted;*
*You drove away the nations and planted it.*
*You cleared the ground for it,*
*and it took root and filled the land....*
*Why have you broken down its walls,*
*so that every passer-by plucks its fruit,*
*The boar from the forest lays it waste,*
*and the beasts of the field feed upon it?*
*Once again, O Lord of hosts,*
*look down from heaven, and see;*
*Take care of this vine,*
*and protect what your right hand has planted.*[3]

Are we who are the Lord's planting in the new dispensation, who possess the promised Christ and His deeper revelation of the Father's love, more dependable, more fruitful than the vineyard of the time of the prophets? If we consider some of the ills of our times—wars; injustices in our racial, business, social, international relationships; the contrast between our Christian profession of spiritual values and our materialistic actions—the words of Isaiah seem so very relevant to us *today:*

*He looked for judgment, but see, bloodshed!*
*for justice, but hark, the outcry!*[4]

## II Give Them Another Chance

There is so much agonizing doubt raised by today's rapid and drastic changes, among God's People as well as in society generally, that sometimes we may be tempted to think that the Lord is finally bringing down on His vineyard the destruction that He threatened. Still we must not fail in the humble but bold trust that the holy ones of Israel showed toward God. For His vineyard, these are times of pain but also, hopefully, times of downpour of the freshening rains of the Holy Spirit, consoling us in the hope of a good harvest even as we cringe at the accompanying winds and thunder.

The Providence of the Father and the power of Christ still care for His Church, His chosen vineyard, upholding its authority, above all renewing its life in the spirit of Vatican II.

*May your help be with the man of your right hand,*
*with the son of man whom you yourself made strong.*
*Then we will no more withdraw from you;*
*give us* new life, *and we will call upon your name.*
*O Lord of hosts, restore us;*
*if your face shine upon us, then we shall be safe.*[5]

1. Is. 5:2 (first reading, A)
2. Is. 5:3-6 (first reading, A)
3. Ps. 80:9-10, 13-16 (responsorial psalm, A)
4. Is. 5:7 (first reading, A)
5. Ps. 80:18-20 (responsorial psalm, A)

## Twenty-eighth Sunday of the Year

Read Wis. 7:7-11
Mk.10:17-27
Ps. 90:12-17
(B)

### I Wisdom the Treasure

The first reading is a praise of wisdom personified, desirable above all else. No riches can compare with her, no power or prestige.

> *Beyond health and comeliness I loved her....*
> *Yet all good things together came to me in her company....*[1]

Wisdom is seeing and choosing the way to life. It comes from God, leads us to Him. In the word of God, wisdom is more than understanding; it involves the affections, possesses the heart. Solomon prays,

> *Give your servant, therefore, an understanding heart...to distinguish right from wrong.*[2]

Our mother Eve wanted to discern between good and evil without the wisdom of God's word, listening to the tempter:

> *...you will be like gods who know what is good and what is bad.*[3]

The wise man examines and tests all things, embracing the good and rejecting the evil. He is always praying to be confirmed and enlarged in wisdom because she has already given some understanding of the realities of life.

*Teach us to number our days aright,*
*that we may gain wisdom of heart.*[4]

How few the days: sometimes when we are young the days seem to move slowly because we have an immediate goal which we long for. As we get older we are increasingly impressed with the shortness of our life, the speed with which the days and years slip away. A visit to the Egyptian section of a museum, where we look at the mummified bodies that were as alive as we ourselves—but five or six thousand years ago—may impress us with the disproportion in the time we shall live and the time we shall be dead. But, believing in an after-life and a final resurrection of our bodies, the sadness of inevitable death is dispelled. Then each short day is a gift, an opportunity, to be welcomed with joy.

*Fill us at daybreak with your kindness,*
*that we may shout for joy and gladness all our days.*[5]

In the Gospel (B) we observe a searching, upright young man whose heart was not yet possessed by the wisdom that could lead him to choose the close following of Christ at the cost of his wealth.

*"Go and sell what you have...come and follow me."*[6]

Only one thing is lacking, but what a demand it made upon him: that he give away everything and follow Christ in utter insecurity. It seems that prudence would have counseled him to sell all but enough to live on in reasonable comfort; or to give the proceeds of the sale into the common fund that would support all the disciples following Jesus. But divine wisdom says simply, get rid of it and follow the Lord in labor and poverty. He went away sad, and left Jesus sad; and we are left wondering about the final fate of this potential apostle because of the haunting words that followed him:

> *"How hard it is for the rich to enter the kingdom of God!"*

## II Wisdom of the Word

The word of God is a power working wisdom in men. Resorting to it frequently, we will find that like a skilled surgeon it lays open our soul, exposing its secret operations and any hidden pathological condition, in order to heal.

> *Indeed, God's word is living and effective, sharper than any two-edged sword. It penetrates and divides soul and spirit, joints and marrow; it judges the reflections and thoughts...all lies bare and exposed....*[7]

The Old Testament makes use of literary personification of wisdom, who is given divine attributes. In New Testament theology, Jesus Himself is Wisdom, a *Christ* [*who is*] *the power of God and the wisdom of God.*[8] The Word is the one complete expression of God's wisdom and knowledge. We listen, but we do not have ears to comprehend. In faith, we try to appreciate an aria from the thundering symphony which includes every note of being. Our eyes search behind the human eyes of the Word enfleshed, and find an ocean-depth of spirit. In our thirst to know, to encompass, we are like a bee floating on a twig near the shore and trying to drink up the sea; or a little fish darting about in exploration of its small area of coral, constantly drawing in the water, receiving life but exhausting nothing.

O Jesus, open our hearts to wisdom—to You—that we may always drink with joy from the fountain of living water which is Your heart.

1. Wis. 7:10, 11 (first reading, B)
2. 1 Kgs. 3:9
3. Gn. 3:5
4. Ps. 90:12 (responsorial psalm, B)
5. Ps. 90:14
6. Mk. 10:21
7. Heb. 4:12-13 (second reading, B)
8. 1 Cor. 1:24

## Twenty-ninth Sunday of the Year

Read Ps. 33:4-5, 18-22
(B)

### I Kindness of the Lord

The responsorial psalm (B) emphasizes "the kindness of the Lord." Another translation uses "love" rather than "kindness." Kindness is the constant attitude of love. We are invited to see, to really understand, the kindness of the Lord, both in the gift of all the good and beautiful creatures surrounding us and in our redemption by the sufferings of Christ.

*Of the kindness of the Lord the earth is full.*[1]

The Lord's love—His constant kindness—does truly fill the earth, but we must view it through the eyes of faith. By faith we know that we were created through love, given a distinct and unique personality, placed in a world full of useful and beautiful things. Without an active faith, we can pass through it all without seeing God's giving and God's presence in evidence everywhere. We may accept all the things and persons that touch our lives as interesting accidents rather than gifts of a loving Father.

### II Hope

It is knowledge of God's faithfulness and kindness that engenders hope, a hope for all the true necessities of this life and especially for redemption and eternal life.

*...see, the eyes of the Lord are upon those who fear him,*
*upon those who hope for his kindness.*[2]

We hope, not because of something in us (and really our own) that makes it fitting that God should regard us, but only because of His fatherly love. We are confident of His mercy and kindness *because* we rely on it.

This kindness of God leads Him to send His Son to sacrifice Himself for our sins. When hope is most difficult, in times of anxiety and fear, of pain or loss, we have an additional motive for hope in the redeeming act of God's Son. Moreover, Jesus, our great high priest, has experienced all the sufferings that might possibly come upon any of us. He is not only the Suffering Servant who has taken our faults upon Himself (first reading), but one who has felt our weaknesses and knows our needs.

*...one who was tempted in every way that we are, yet never sinned. So let us confidently approach the throne of grace to receive mercy and favor....*[3]

*May your kindness, O Lord, be upon us*
*who have put our hope in you.*[4]

## III Gratitude and Service

Gratitude is the natural response to love and kindness.

*Enter his gates with thanksgiving,*
*his courts with praise;*

*Give thanks to him; bless his name, for he is good:*
*the Lord, whose kindness endures forever,*
*and his faithfulness, to all generations.*[5]

Gratitude is expressed most truly in doing. Jesus expressed His love for us in service; He expects us to show our grateful love in the same way. In the Gospel story the brothers James and John ask the favor of being very close to their Master when He comes into His glory: to sit at His right and His left hand. The other disciples are indignant when they hear of it. Jesus calls them together and explains that those who will have authority in His Church must follow His own example, aiming to be first in service rather than in honor and power.

*Anyone among you who aspires to greatness must serve the rest; whoever wants to rank first among you must serve the needs of all. The Son of Man has not come to be served but to serve—to give his life in ransom for the many.*[6]

Lord Jesus, from Your life we see two ways to give our lives to You who have given Yours for us. We can very practically serve the needs of others; and we can help them by bearing any pain or sorrow which Your providence sends us, sharing Your suffering, with Your intention that "many may be justified." Lord, teach me to give my life in service, as You gave Your life in service and suffering for us.

1. Ps. 33:5
2. Ps. 33:18
3. Heb. 4:15-16 (second reading)
4. Ps. 33:22
5. Ps. 100:4-5
6. Mk. 10:43-45

## Thirtieth Sunday of the Year

Read Jer. 31:7-9
Heb. 5:1-6
Mk. 10:46-52
(B)

# I Thus Says the Lord: Shout with Joy[1]

We are given in this Sunday's readings several reasons for joy and gratitude: that the Lord has saved His people; has given us the priesthood through which He continues His presence and work among us; and through faith has cured our blindness, given us a new vision of ourselves and of the universe.

> The Lord has done great things for us;
> we are filled with joy.[2]

Joy belongs to the believer in Christ above all men. Not that the Redeemer has eliminated sorrows, restraints and pains. Rather He has made them the means of joy, freedom and fullness of life. He has transformed death, that ultimate horror, the inescapable exit to nothingness, into a door to fullness of being in life everlasting.

In creating man free, God necessarily became judge, and this is a sobering prospect; but He chose to be above all a Father.

> *...I am a father to Israel,*
> *Ephraim is my first-born.*[3]

We are captives to sin, to the disordered passions within us, but in Christ our Father frees us:

*When the Lord brought back the captives of Zion,*
*we were like men dreaming.*
*Then our mouth was filled with laughter,*
*and our tongue with rejoicing.*[4]

## II Chosen and Commissioned

*It was not you who chose me,*
*it was I who chose you*
*to go forth and bear fruit.*[5]

God's people have respect for their priests, and for their bishops, the high priests of the New Covenant, because they have been *taken from among men and made their representative before God.... One does not take this honor on his own initiative, but only when called by God....*[6]

In these days of specialized education and realistic examination of credentials, there is no longer that simplicity of the faithful that expected the priest to have a solution for every human problem. There should still be a confidence in his relative competency, in view of his training, in the areas of the Church's moral and doctrinal teaching, though here too he cannot always have definite answers to every problem. The wise priest is ready to admit that he is sometimes confused by the differences of opinion among today's most popular theological writers. Still, because of his office, the Holy Spirit assists him in his direction of others. It should help us have easy communication with a priest to remember that *he is able to deal patiently with erring sinners, for he himself is beset by weakness....*[7]

There is mutual strengthening and encouragement in a trusting communication between the priest and his people.

## III ...That I May See

Jesus gave sight to the blind man who sought it persistently in spite of the fact that *many people were scolding him to make him keep quiet.... "Your faith has healed you."*[8]

Faith gives clearer sight, eyes that penetrate beyond first flat impressions, that perceive depth, perspective and the rich harmonies of form, texture, color. We see things a little as God sees them, their significance and purpose. We see as the goal of creation all humanity united in love and in Christ, for the glory of the Creator.

*God saw how good it was.*[9] Lord God, let me see that it is very good, all that You have made, that composite of things, persons and events touching upon my life—and that life itself. It is only my misuse that is evil, and detracts from the glory that creation gives You.

*Great are the works of the Lord,*
*exquisite in all their delights.*
*Majesty and glory are his work,*
*and his justice endures forever.*[10]

1. Jer. 31:7 (first reading, B)
2. Responsorial psalm
3. Jer. 31:9
4. Ps. 126:1-2 (responsorial psalm, B)
5. Jn. 15:16
6. Heb. 5:1, 4 (second reading, B)
7. Heb. 5:2
8. Cf. Mk. 10:46-52 (Gospel, B)
9. Gn. 1:25
10. Ps. 111:2-3

Thirtieth Sunday of the Year

(Alternate)

## See Your Optometrist

One of our greatest health-care needs is for good spiritual optometrists. Every one of us has a congenital defect in his spiritual sight. It is an unusual phenomenon, for we are both near-sighted and far-sighted.

Concerning flaws and defects, we are far-sighted. With eyes on ourselves, it is very difficult to discern defects, and they seem rather small and indistinct. Looking at others, we see such defects very clearly, in great detail.

When we are looking for good and noble characteristics, we are near-sighted. Our own virtues stand out sharply and larger than life. Considering others, they may seem a bit fuzzy and rather reduced in size.

Perhaps rarely we *do* get help from such an optometrist: a courageous friend, a knowing and frank spiritual adviser, or even an ill-disposed critic.

Our vision can be greatly helped by better light. We need the Holy Spirit, who is Fire—a clean flame that gives both light of knowledge and warmth of love. In His light we can search out what we have ignored or simply not seen in the dark places of our soul. In His warmth we can love others in a manner that excludes minute critical examination.

*Why look at the speck in your brother's eye when you miss the plank in your own?*[1]

*Rabboni, I want to see.*[2]

1. Mt. 7:3
2. Mk. 10:51 (Gospel, B)

## Thirty-first Sunday of the Year

Read Wis. 11:23–12:2
Ps. 145:10-11
(C)

The sun was shining brightly on this August morning. The temperature was perfect. But I noted only one bird darting silently into a mangled tree. And my heart was chilled.

All about me lay what seemed symbols of God's wrath and the desolation of sin. The damage of a tornado can be appalling, and this had been one of the worst.

I could not subdue the persistent idea that here was an image of what was happening to the Church. Pope John had opened windows in the Church; it needed some fresh breezes to sweep out the air that had been thickening for centuries. But suddenly—a tornado!

Giant beeches were down, their clean white trunks lying in the mud like fallen chastity. Great oaks, figure of enduring strength, were uprooted from their deep moorings in the earth. Hard trunks of maples had been shattered by the fury from the black clouds. Some of these venerable trees revealed a decay and hollowness that had not been evident before. But others, both very old and quite young, had been perfectly sound, but had snapped in this one wild moment of nature's passion.

*Have pity on me, O God; have pity on me,*
*for in you I take refuge.*
*In the shadow of your wings I take refuge,*
*till harm pass by.*[1]

All this destruction I found on the Novitiate grounds—if not more severe than elsewhere, at least more striking. At the shrine I was very sad. It had been a place to pray easily for my dear ones; but also, because of its expansive background of wooded hills and sky, for *all* the children of the Mother of the Church. Mary lay on her face on the hard pavement that had felt the light and the heavy tread of innumerable feet of those who had found her both joy and strength. I wondered pessimistically if she would ever be put back on the pedestal. Perhaps Venus or Aphrodite might replace her more properly in this culture which so exploits nudity and sex.

Still, the sun was shining brilliantly. And the sun had been the chief source of the energy that had created this beautiful wooded area. There were many trees still standing, though some would forever exhibit the scars of their terrible testing. The rustle of their leaves in gentle breezes would still whisper gratitude for their *being*, and for the sunshine and rains that had in the past, and would in in the future, express God's providence.

*...who can resist the might of your arm...?*
*But you have mercy on all, because you can*
*do all things;*
*and you overlook the sins of men that they*
*may repent.*
*For you love all things that are*
*and loathe nothing that you have made;*

*for what you hated, you would not have fashioned.*
*And how could a thing remain, unless you willed it;*
*or be preserved, had it not been called forth by you?*
*But you spare all things, because they*
*are yours, O Lord and lover of souls,*
*for your imperishable spirit is in all things!*
*Therefore you rebuke offenders little by little,*
*warn them, and remind them of the sins they are committing,*
*that they may abandon their wickedness and believe in you, O Lord!*[2]

1. Ps. 57:2
2. Wis. 11:21, 23-26; 12:1-2 (first reading, C)

## Thirty-second Sunday of the Year

Read Mk. 12:38-44
1 Kgs. 17:10-16
(B)

### I Widow and Pharisee

In these readings we have praise of widows, generous, trusting and poor; and denunciation of Pharisees, phony lovers of honor and praise. The widows were sincere servants of the Lord; the Pharisees, insincere and self-satisfied.

In the first reading we hear of God's providence caring for a widow who trusts in Him and His prophet. The responsorial psalm sings of God's love for such:

> *Who keeps faith forever,*
> *secures justice for the oppressed,*
> *gives food to the hungry.*
> *...the fatherless and the widow he sustains....*[1]

In the Gospel we meet the scribes and Pharisees, who love honor and deference, make show of piety with long prayers, but forget justice in dealing with the poor. They are threatened with severe judgment.[2]

In a reading of the previous Sunday (Gospel, A) we have similar criticism of scribes and Pharisees recorded by another evangelist:

*They bind up heavy loads, hard to carry, to lay on other shoulders, while they themselves will not lift a finger to budge them. All their works are performed to be seen.*[3]

It has always been a sad, scandalous thing when those who are legitimate religious leaders do not give example of what they preach. Yet generally they have offered the word of God and right moral direction. While there is a great natural urge to disregard the counsel and teaching of such insincere (sometimes merely weak) leaders, the Lord directs that their official position be respected and honored by humble obedience.

*"The scribes and the Pharisees have succeeded Moses as teachers; therefore do everything and observe everything they tell you. But do not follow their example. Their words are bold but their deeds are few."*[4]

## II Giving All We Have

Jesus sat down near the treasury and saw the people putting their offerings into it, some much and others less. As a poor widow came along and dropped in two small coins, He said to His disciples,

*"...this poor widow contributed more than all the others who donated to the treasury. They gave from their surplus wealth, but she gave from her want, all that she had to live on."*[5]

Just as we cannot judge the true worth in God's eyes of a financial offering, neither can we make comparisons of generosity and self-giving in general. A man of great natural talent or the recipient of special graces may be doing some striking work for the Church or for humanity. Yet it may not measure up to what he might accomplish, because of some degree of indolence or selfishness. The efforts of another, producing no observable effect on the world or even his own little life-circle, may be the best he is capable of, and in God's eyes the generous offering of the widow's penny.

> *More will be asked of a man to whom more has been entrusted.*[6]

As in the case of the poor widow, Christ's admiration and love go out to those who offer to God everything they possess, "all they have to live on":

the cleverness of their minds
the stored treasures of their memories
the hard-won fruits of their education and experience
the skill of their hands
the compassion of their hearts —
and sometimes, *patience* with their *lack* of talent, or health and energy.

Lord Jesus, I wish to give You all that I have, my whole living. I want to give it in gratitude; in complete trust in Your providence; for the good of others who may be poorer even than I. What I can give may seem nothing; but if it is all I have, to You it will be much. And You will take my gift, unite it to the infinite treasures of Your heart and offer it to the Father for the saving of men.

1. Ps. 146:6-7, 9
2. Cf. Mk. 12:38-40
3. Mt. 23:4-5
4. Mt. 23:2-4
5. Mk. 12:43-44 (Gospel)
6. Lk. 12:48

## Thirty-third Sunday of the Year

Read Lk. 21:5-19
(B)

# I Destruction and Judgment

The readings (B and C) for this Sunday at the close of the year refer to the end of the world, the culmination of history and the fulfillment of God's purpose in creating man and the world in which he was placed. In the first reading (B) we hear the prophet Daniel:

*It shall be a time unsurpassed in distress*
*since nations began until that time.*
*At that time your people shall escape,*
*everyone who is found written in the book.*
*Many of those who sleep*
*in the dust of the earth shall awake;*
*Some shall live forever,*
*others shall be an everlasting horror and disgrace.*[1]

Then from Mark we have the words of Jesus:

*...the sun will be darkened, the moon will not shed its light,...the heavenly hosts will be shaken. Then men will see the Son of Man coming in the clouds with great power and glory. He will dispatch his angels and assemble his chosen....*[2]

The infant Church had to grow in knowledge of who Christ was, His relationship to history and to eternity. It needed also to develop a balance between two aspects of its character, the eschatological and the incarnational. Christ was in the world, very much a man concerned with men's needs and sufferings; teaching justice and practical love. Yet He also transcended this here and now of earth and time, pointing to an end of history and to a world to come.

## II Renewal and Salvation

The Scripture readings for this Sunday indicate *destruction* of the world and *judgment*. But other passages tell rather of *renewal* and *salvation*.

> *...the world itself will be freed from its slavery to corruption and share in the glorious freedom of the children of God. Yes, we know that all creation groans and is in agony even until now. Not only that, but we ourselves, although we have the Spirit as first fruits, groan inwardly while we await the redemption of our bodies.*[3]

Paul sees the physical world as being redeemed and sharing man's destiny, even as it had shared the disorder brought by his sin. Man abused nature through his dominion over it, but it was to be restored as was man himself, through Christ, for the glory of the Creator.

> *I come to gather nations of every language;*
> *they shall come and see my glory.*
> *As the new heavens and the new earth*
> *which I will make*

*Shall endure before me, says the Lord,*
*so shall your race and your name endure.*[4]

For those keenly aware of the deterioration of the earth through thoughtless and selfish exploitation—the wholesale pollution of air and water, the unnecessary destruction of much natural beauty—the need for redemption and restoration of both man and his environment is very apparent. The question arises, are we not required by God to work now, with all our resources, towards the redeeming of the physical world as well as our own souls? God will probably not restore and perfect the earth, as He will not redeem us, without our own efforts and cooperation.

If there is sin in stealing from or damaging the property of an *individual,* what of the damage to the ecology which affects every human person on this earth and the generations to come?

*Then I saw new heavens and a new earth....*
*This is God's dwelling among men.*[5]

Lord Jesus, while we wait for Your coming and the renewal of our sin-damaged souls and of all creation, help us to do our part in this universal redemption. Give us the constant desire to work patiently to conform our hearts to Your own perfect heart. Help us to deal with all the things about us with the reverence they deserve as the gift of Your Father to us and to His children of all future generations. Come, Lord Jesus, and restore us and all things to the perfection which will properly glorify the infinite Creator who is our Father.

1. Dn. 12:1-2
2. Mk. 13:24-27 (Gospel, B)
3. Rom. 8:21-23
4. Is. 66:18, 22
5. Cf. Rv. 21:1-3

## Thirty-fourth Sunday of the Year
## Christ the King

Read Jn. 18:33-37
Rv. 1:5-8

### I King of Glory

In our atmosphere of democracy, freedom and personalism, some of the words we find in today's liturgy, when applied to heads of state, have an archaic ring: sovereignty, majesty, glory and power. Our modern equivalent of kings receive no humble reverence or unquestioning submission, but are considered as servants of the people, open to criticism and even rejection. The personal imperfections of these public servants, and any failings in office, proven or suspected, are unmercifully exposed by the news media, to the detriment of respect for both their person and their authority.

It is fitting that these words of the liturgy should be reserved for the honoring of Jesus Christ, whether we think of Him as king, president, ruler, or leader. He *is* Lord, and alone shares with God His Father absolute sovereignty and infinite majesty, glory and power. It is only to that Son of Man who bears the perfection of divinity that complete submission and unreserved reverence are properly given by free man.

*He received dominion, glory and kingship;*
*nations and peoples of every language serve him.*[1]

## II Judge

Man does indeed possess great dignity and freedom, which must be respected by those who govern. But some men would extend liberty to include freedom to sin—which is really loss of both freedom and dignity. We best see this in certain evil habits which can so possess man's thoughts and desires that he loses his ability to function as an intelligent, self-determining person. Our actions are always limited by our conscience. As Catholics, our conscience is formed through knowledge of the fundamental message of Christ in the Gospels and in humble deference to the Church's interpretation of it. Since this message is summed up in the twofold command of love, conscience will be largely concerned with personal, social relationships.

Conscience gives a here-and-now judgment, in the light of the teaching of the Church, my past experience, and my growth in understanding, of a particular action as it relates to love of God and man. This judgment is made with the guidance of the Holy Spirit and His gift of counsel.

Our conscience often directs us to difficult ways, and we fail to follow it. But dignity is restored by our Savior-King. *Through him we have redemption, for forgiveness of our sins.*[2]

It is to Jesus Christ that each man must finally give account for his use of freedom.

> *...and all the nations will be assembled before him. Then he will separate them into two groups, as a shepherd separates sheep from goats.*[3]

## III Suffering King

The Gospel, in contrast to the first reading, presents Jesus as humiliated and on trial before a Roman official, even while He claims kingship, but "not of this world." Can we accept as our leader the "king" who dies in disgrace as a criminal? It is precisely here on the cross that He has earned our complete allegiance as no other leader could. This King ransomed every one of His people, paid for their freedom and happiness by His own death.

> *To him who loves us and freed us from our sins by his own blood...to him be glory and power forever and ever!*[4]

The suffering that is inevitably part of human life will never be completely vanquished; so we shall always need a leader who understands this suffering from experience and who can show us the meaning and value in it. There is universal longing for that ideal world which is uniquely the Kingdom of Christ: "a kingdom of justice, love and peace."[5] We can hardly hope to see in our lifetime this humanity of so many diverse interests and philosophies united in perfect harmony and brotherhood. But we are called by our Leader to work strenuously toward it. Our hope is in the final triumph of Jesus and His followers in a kingdom not of this world. It was in a time of decimation of believers in bitter persecution that the hymn of triumph found in Revelation was written:

> *The heavens were opened, and as I looked on, a white horse appeared; its rider was called "The Faithful and True." Justice is his standard.... A name was written on the part of the cloak that covered his thigh: "King of kings and Lord of lords."*[6]

Almighty and eternal God, You have renewed all creation in Your beloved Son, the King of the whole universe. May all the peoples of the earth, now torn apart by the wound of sin, become subject to the gentle rule of Your only-begotten Son. Who lives and reigns with You and the Holy Spirit, one God, for ever and ever.[7]

1. Dn. 7:14 (first reading, B)
2. Col. 1:14 (second reading, C)
3. Mt. 25:32 (Gospel, A)
4. Rv. 1:5-6 (second reading, B)
5. Preface
6. Rv. 19:11, 16
7. Opening prayer

## Trinity Sunday

Read Dn. 3:52-82
Mt. 28:16-20
Jn. 16:12-15

### I Holy God

The spirit of today's liturgy is joyful praise of the Triune God. The key word is "Blessed." We bless—praise, honor, reverence and thank—the infinite majesty of God. Self-interest is subdued and all our attention directed in awe and gratitude to the mysterious God who is transcendent, yet immanent; who is One and yet a Community of Persons.

> Blessed be the Holy Trinity, and undivided unity: we will give glory to Him....(Entrance verse).

The mystery of the Trinity is revealed chiefly through Jesus Christ. In the Old Testament God's unity is stressed, and it was faithfulness to this idea of God's oneness that for the most part saved His chosen people from worshiping the many gods of the pagans who surrounded them. Now we are favored with the revelation of the inner life of God which human reason could not discover, any more than the naked eye could search out features in the blazing sun. Faith accepts this revelation with delight.

## 11 Knowing, Loving, Sharing

With the revelation of the Trinity it is impossible to conceive of God as the great lonely One, infinitely removed from our own social form of life. We see an intense life of knowing, loving and sharing of three equal Persons in the one God. All that the Father has belongs to the Son also. The Holy Spirit shares all with the Father and Son.

*...he will give glory to me,*
*because he will have received from me*
*what he will announce to you.*
*All that the Father has belongs to me.*[1]

More easily do we now approach a knowledge of God's bliss, for we have a frame of reference in our own joy in a companionship of sharing what we have, what we know, what we are—in love. We can project, weakly, our small knowledge to God's infinite knowledge, our imperfect love to His perfect love, our partial and changeable happiness to God's absolute, unchanging beatitude. When we have advanced a little in the way of divine love, we find pleasure in *God's* joy and perfections—aside from His goodness to *us*—and make truly our own that phrase in the "Glory to God":

We praise you for your glory!

In this spirit also we can make our own that song of praise in Daniel:

*"Blessed are you, O Lord, the God of our fathers,*
*praiseworthy and exalted above all forever;*
*And blessed is your holy and glorious name....*
*Bless the Lord, all you works of the Lord....*
*You sons of men, bless the Lord:*
*praise and exalt him above all forever....*

*Give thanks to the Lord, for he is good,*
*for his mercy endures forever."*[2]

## III Dedication

We were initiated into the kingdom of God, given a divine life, in the name of the most blessed Trinity.

"...*go, therefore, and make disciples of all the nations.*
*Baptize them in the name*
*'of the Father,*
*and of the Son,*
*and of the Holy Spirit.'* "[3]

We should say with deep reverence that first of the prayers which most of us learned as children and whose meaning we could not grasp, "In the name of the Father and of the Son and of the Holy Spirit." It is an act of faith, a prayer of praise, a dedication. It is thanksgiving for what we owe to each of the three divine Persons.

Thanks to You, Father, simply because You are our Father. Help us to have the attitude of a child towards its father: You know everything; understand all our needs and provide for them; You can do anything. You love us, and so we love and trust You.

Thanks to You, Jesus, the Son, the Word become man, most perfect revelation of God to us. We know the Father by knowing the Son. We will love You who first loved us, and gave such proof of Your love.

Thanks to You, Holy Spirit, the Love of the Father and the Son. Love should evoke love. You are the giver of gifts that are precious above all material things, gifts of understanding, wisdom, strength; and Your gifts produce in us love, joy and peace.

We are specially grateful to You, Most Blessed Trinity, for dwelling within us.

> *"Anyone who loves me will be true to my word,*
> *and my Father will love him;*
> *we will come to him*
> *and make our dwelling place with him."*[4]

> *I will ask the Father*
> *and he will give you another Paraclete—*
> *to be with you always....*[5]

1. Jn. 16:14-15 (Gospel, C)
2. Dn. 3:52, 57, 82, 89
3. Mt. 28:19 (Gospel, B)
4. Jn. 14:23
5. Jn. 14:16

Corpus Christi
(Thursday or Sunday after Trinity Sunday)

Read Heb. 9:11-15

## I Thanksgiving Sacrifice

In the responsorial psalm (B) we have a succinct expression of a twofold aspect of the sacrament of Christ's Body:

*I shall walk before the Lord*
*in the lands of the living....*
*To you will I offer sacrifice of thanksgiving,*
*and I will call upon the name of the Lord.*[1]

Each liturgical celebration of the "eucharist" (thanksgiving) is a perfect thanks-offering. In Christ we have a gift commensurate with the sum of all the gifts we have received from a Father who is infinitely rich and infinitely good. We confidently offer one gift which discharges the great debt we inevitably incur by being Christians, but also by simply *being*, having life from the Creator. We are sustained in that life by an immeasurable composite of blessings: all the intricately balanced conditions of our environment necessary for physical life; the amazing functions, coordination and adaptability of the body; the marvelous mind, its operations rooted in the physical but reaching out in unbounded quest for knowing—grasping, possessing all that exists—searching beyond, to the First Cause, the Beginning, He Who Is.

The sensitive creature—son though he is, or all the more because son—might be overwhelmed by a sense of his debt. But he perfectly discharges it in the one "Sacrifice of thanksgiving," the offering to the Father of Jesus Christ, the beloved Son.

We rejoice in offering ourselves and our whole round earth, wrapped like a gift in its transparent film of atmosphere, together with Christ. All our debts paid, we are free, fully alive. For does not Christ

> *...who through the eternal spirit offered himself up unblemished to God, cleanse our consciences from dead works to worship the living God?*[2]

## II The Lord's Presence

Living in the Church, we *walk before the Lord in the lands of the living.* Separated from God, we walk in a land of death. This idea may easily be eclipsed by the bright, omnipresent images of life from television and the glossy magazines: fullness of life is in the horsepower and chrome of a car; in the taste of alcohol of this label, a drink of spiced and gassed water; in a credit card; in a body deodorized, creamed and well decorated. Life is in movement, change, experiences; in luxury surroundings, gourmet food, easy sex.

All these things can be "life" in the land of death, where God is ignored. In the Land of the Living, where we walk in the Lord's presence, none of them are necessary. If they were, many would have no real chance to live.

God the Father is the principle of life. We have received His life through the Son; and in a special way through that union effected by the sacrament of His body and blood.

> *"Just as the Father who has life sent me*
> *and I have life because of the Father,*
> *so the man who feeds on me*
> *will have life because of me.*
> *This is the bread that came down from heaven.*
> *Unlike your ancestors who ate and died nonetheless,*
> *the man who feeds on this bread shall live forever."*[3]

The representation of life in our "consumerism syndrome" can lead us to totally selfish pursuit of needs. Life in Christ demands self-giving, loving the other as the self, because each is a member of the same body, whose life is diminished by diminution in any least part of that body. "Communion" is the very apt expression of this life, embracing God, ourselves, each other, in fellowship, sharing, communication of life.

> *Is not the cup of blessing we bless a sharing in the blood of Christ? And is not the bread we break a sharing in the body of Christ? Because the loaf of bread is one, we, many though we are, are one body, for we all partake of the one loaf.*[4]

Jesus, make us hunger for the Bread of Life!

1. Ps. 116:9, 17
2. Heb. 9:14 (second reading, B)
3. Jn. 6:57-58 (Gospel, A)
4. 1 Cor. 10:16-17 (second reading, A)

Sacred Heart
(Friday of the Second Week
After Pentecost)

Read Ex. 3:1-6
1 Jn. 4:7-16

## I God is Power

When we consider the universe visible to us in night's darkness, God's power and unlimited creativity stagger our minds. We wrestle with the facts astronomers are able to give us, but are overwhelmed by the limitless spaces, masses and energies. We have managed, with a mighty and extremely expensive technology, to have man put foot on the moon after thousands of years of scanning the heavens, wondering, calculating and dreaming. This moon is comparatively within arm's length. We look with awe at our sun, the tiniest fraction of whose total light and heat strikes our earth but can blind the eyes and torture the body while nearly a hundred million miles distant. And this sun—864,000 miles in diameter, 10,000 degrees fahrenheit on its surface—is an insignificant body measured against many of the other stars visible to the naked eye, to say nothing of the galaxy of which it is a part, a mass of stars swinging around a hub in a diameter of 600 million billion miles. We are told that the star Deneb, speck in the sky, is actually 63,000 times as bright as the sun, though 1630 light years distant.

> *The heavens declare the glory of God,*
> *and the firmament proclaims his handiwork.*[1]

Yet God infinitely transcends all His wondrous works:

> *Of old you established the earth,*
> *and the heavens are the work of your hands.*
> *They shall perish, but you remain*
> *though all of them grow old like a garment.*
> *Like clothing you change them and they are changed,*
> *but you are the same, and your years have no end.*[2]

## II God is Holiness

When God revealed Himself, Moses was told to take off his shoes in approaching, as he was in a holy place. *Moses hid his face, for he was afraid to look at God.*[3] When he was called to the top of the mountain to receive God's commandments, the people were warned not to pass certain limits near the sacred place.

> *When the people witnessed the thunder and lightening, the trumpet blast and the mountain smoking, they all feared and trembled. So they took up a position much farther away.... "...God has come to you only to test you and put his fear upon you, lest you should sin."*[4]

The chosen people had their "holy place," and the "Holy of Holies,"

*...only the high priest went into the inner one (tabernacle), and that but once a year....*[5]

## III God is Love!

The apostle John had enjoyed a most intimate companionship with God-made-man, from the first meeting when he was invited to see where Jesus lived, *and stayed with him that day,*[6] to the last cruel vigil by the cross with the Lord's mother. There he watched a soldier's lance lay open the heart of Christ. In his old age he summed up his knowledge of God: God is Love.

*God is love,*
*and he who abides in love*
*abides in God and God in him.*[7]

This love demands response. But how can we love, when *no one has ever seen God*[8]—the almighty Creator, the absolutely Holy and Perfect, *who dwells in unapproachable light?*[9]

Since God sent His only Son into the world, His love is made palpable, human, and easy for us. We understand in the symbol of Jesus' heart the love of His Father. St. John, in what, standing alone, seems a *non sequitur,* tells us how we should love God:

*Beloved,*
*if God has loved us so,*
*we must have the same love for one another.*[10]

We would expect, "we must have the same love for God," but he says "one another." So I love the Father, I love Christ, by loving Christ's brother walking the street with me, working with me, living in my neighborhood—and possibly opposing me or something I hold precious or sacred. Loving thus, I live in God and God lives in me.

O Father of Glory, give us the grace, through Your Spirit, to grow strong in faith, so that Christ may live in us; strong in knowledge of Christ above all knowledge; filled with the love of His heart, which is Your own perfect love.

1. Ps. 19:2
2. Ps. 102:26-28
3. Ex. 3:6
4. Ex. 20:18, 20
5. Heb. 9:7
6. Jn. 1:39
7. 1 Jn. 4:16 (second reading, A)
8. 1 Jn. 4:12
9. 1 Tm. 6:16
10. 1 Jn. 4:11 (second reading, A)

## Joseph, Husband of Mary
(March 19)

Read Mt. 1:16-24
Lk. 2:41-51

Joseph, what a privileged relationship is yours: companion and husband of the one chosen, singled out by the Creator from all the fair women who have graced the earth since Eve, mother of all. In pursuit of her image, painters and sculptors compete and poets despair; for who can capture the unique, unexperienced perfection of the woman *so highly favored,*[1] "our tainted nature's solitary boast"?[2]

And what is it like, Joseph, to be known as father of a child you must reverence, whom adults must kneel to; who as a boy of twelve would prove Master among doctors of divinity? To be teacher of a craft to one who would teach all men about life in its fullness? To be thus related to one who came late in the progress of humanity from its cradling in the mists of antiquity but whose appearance caused men to begin anew the numbering of their historical annals? To direct as parent one to whom all the holy men of the ages would yield place, like His cousin the Baptist, because *the one who comes after me ranks ahead of me, for he was before me?*[3] As an instructed Jew, you knew that no one has ever seen God. Yet you are privileged to study daily the human face of one who would be proclaimed *the only Son, ever at the Father's side, who has revealed him.*[4]

It is this heavenly Father who asked you to be stand-in, to care for His Son visiting among us. Even in your dreams you were alert to His voice, helping you in your immediate problems—which concerned, ultimately, plans for saving the world. You were one of those blessed ones, Joseph, who hear the word of God and keep it.

It seems to us unfortunate that you are a silent figure in the Scriptures, you who could speak more eloquently than all theologians, painters and poets about Mary, paragon of virgins, wives, and mothers, who was your dear daily companion. And about Jesus, in whose mysterious presence you lived. It is said of you and Mary that you did not understand. Your understanding was a slow dawning of the light that was to enlighten all men. Help us to see and rejoice in a light that still must grow and overpower the darkness about us.

Mary, you could have told us about Joseph, man of unselfish love, sensitive listener to the divine voice. We study the carpenter of Nazareth—who as your husband was known as the father of Jesus—so to see better the earthiness and brotherly closeness to us of the Son of the living God. And looking at Jesus in a carpenter's shop, we understand better the dignity of Joseph the workman.

Holy Spirit, it is only You who can reveal to us the rare beauty of human persons transformed by total surrender to Your divine direction. Show us how our own Nazareth of dull, common duties can be a God-planned life in the companionship of Jesus.

*Happy they who dwell in your house!*
*continually they praise you.*[5]

1. Cf. Lk. 1:28
2. William Wordsworth, "The Virgin"
3. Jn. 1:15
4. Jn. 1:18
5. Ps. 84:5 (Gospel acclamation)

## Annunciation
## (March 25)

Read Lk. 1:26-38

*Mary said, "I am the servant of the Lord. Let it be done to me as you say."*[1]

Mary, you respond to God's proposal,
through His angel of the Good News,
by entire commitment.
A pledge of fidelity that made possible
the saving of a ruined world;
that was firm foundation
for God's building of a new heaven and a new earth.

Your fiat, Blessed Mother, is your life-program:
"Servant of the Lord."
Personal fulfillment—
that is all wrapped up in a passion
for the transcendent will of God
and the urgent need of others.

You are bright witness of vows fulfilled,
even in the deepest pain;
of promises kept,
for the saving of a human society
entirely dependent upon *fidelity*,
in God,
and in man.

*Your word, O Lord, endures forever;*
*it is firm as the heavens.*
*Through all generations your truth endures;*
*you have established the earth and it stands firm.*
*According to your ordinances they still stand firm;*
*all things serve you.*
*Had not your law been my delight,*
*I should have perished in my affliction.*[2]

1. Lk. 1:38 (Gospel)
2. Ps. 119:89-92

When Gabriel shattered your silent prayer
with news of a Son you were chosen to bear—
the Lord, who from glory in heaven now stole
and softly knocked at the door of your soul—
the earth, all expectant, rejoiced at your word:
"I am the servant of the Lord."

And then in secret of Bethlehem's night,
poor Joseph so anguished at seeing your plight
(in spite of the work he had frantically done
'twas a wretched welcome to offer this Son),
was it harder that night for your heart to accord
with "I am the servant of the Lord"?

And now that appointed, bitter day
when powers of darkness hold their sway,
and waves of hot passion surge and toss
round our Mother of Sorrows who stands by the cross:
how noble, at thrust of Simeon's sword,
this "I am the servant of the Lord"!

## Joseph the Worker
## (May 1 or Labor Day)

Read Gn. 1:26—2:3
Col. 3:17, 23-24

# I Hard Labor

Jesus was known as "the carpenter's son." And He Himself did the same work in the years at Nazareth, as Mark indicates: *Is this not the carpenter, the son of Mary...?*[1] He sanctified the labor of hands by engaging in it before He began His intellectual and spiritual work.

Work has two very different aspects: a necessary evil, or a privileged activity. One is that of something imposed or at least become difficult as a result of sin:

> *"Cursed be the ground because of you!*
> *In toil shall you eat its yield*
> *all the days of your life.*
> *Thorns and thistles shall it bring forth to you,*
> *as you eat of the plants of the field.*
> *By the sweat of your face*
> *shall you get bread to eat...."*[2]

Our labors are at times a physical burden, a tedious routine, usually only partly successful or satisfying. Adam was to support himself with the remarkable variety of the earth's fruitfulness and natural resources, as are we today, but now under less than ideal circumstances. Labor in this light, done in faith and patience, becomes a reparation for sin, an expression of contrite love.

## II Creative Activity

Work has a dignity and joy because it is a sharing by man in the continuing work of creation, the development of the world. A loving Father permits His sons to help Him in His work. Through work, man expresses his God-given dominion over creation.

> *Then God said, "Let us make man in our image, after our likeness. Let them have dominion over the fish of the sea, the birds of the air, and the cattle, and over all the wild animals and all the creatures that crawl on the ground. "...fill the earth and subdue it."*[3]

It is given to man to form and shape and transmute material creation according to his needs; and beyond that, to satisfy the restless search of his intellect for knowledge of the mysterious world about him. Work takes its dignity from its likeness to the activity of the Creator.

> *My Father is at work until now,*
> *and I am at work as well.*[4]

There are human activities obviously noble in that they engage the best intelligences to transform materials and energies of creation, or directly influence and perfect man himself. But all work possesses an essential dignity.

A man digging a ditch for a pipe, or hauling mortar, or seeding a lawn has a share in building the city of man.

The barber, laundry woman, hair stylist, seamstress, plumber, school janitor, shoeshine boy, are all helping to keep order and beauty in our world.

The nurse and orderly, the teacher, the physician and dentist, the housekeeper, the salad chef and dish washer, all are serving man himself, and, with a directed intention, are exercising *love,* the transformer of the universe.

## III Gift of a New Day

It is unfortunate that many of us do not naturally shake off sleep and weariness quickly, to greet a new day with the exuberance it deserves; that we cannot feel the excitement of the poet with a clean pad on which to record a fresh vision; of the painter with a new canvas who has come upon a fascinating perspective. With the new day we are given a new beginning, a renewed potential, a gift of love from the Creator.

*Fill us at daybreak with your kindness,*
*that we may shout for joy and gladness all our days.*[5]

There are mornings when our first thought may be for an aspirin rather than a song. Yet this joy for a new day is not dependent on perfect physical well-being, or on a mind tranquilized by freedom from problems or ignorance of the evils of our times. It is the Easter joy of the people of the resurrection. "Alleluia is our song!"

*Let your work be seen by your servants*
*and your glory by their children.*[6]

Heavenly Father, through Jesus Your Son, I joyfully offer You my day: its prayers, hopes, and disappointments; its work and leisure; its joys and sorrows. Let me praise You as Jesus, Joseph and Mary praised You each day of their own simple living at Nazareth.

1. Mk. 6:3
2. Gn. 3:17-19
3. Gn. 1:26, 28 (first reading)
4. Jn. 5:17
5. Ps. 90:14 (responsorial psalm)
6. Ps. 90:16 (responsorial psalm)

## Joseph the Worker (Alternate)
## (May 1 or Labor Day)

In a corner of the seminary grounds there lay an unsightly heap: many minor parts of car bodies, pieces of wire and metal, a discarded fan—a most miscellaneous pile of junk. It was the source material for a blowtorch sculptor who could sort out items from this miniature dump, weld them together, and turn out a work of art.

Our lives are cluttered with large amounts of junk: trivial involvements that have become our routine week after week; seemingly useless activities and aggravations; things misshapen, corroded, downright ugly. Of what value in our spiritual life, of what apostolic usefulness is this daily accretion of junk in our lives? The Christian of living faith becomes creative and has the power to weld together something meaningful and beautiful from what seems useless and mean.

Welding requires oxygen, iron and fire. God the Creator gives us oxygen: the breath of life, life intelligent and spiritual. His Holy Spirit supplies the iron of fortitude and the fire of divine love. With these we can create what is attractive and inspiring to discerning men. Our lives can reflect the beauty of Christ's human life, manifesting the glory of the Father.

> *Whatever you do, work at it with your whole being. Do it for the Lord rather than for men, since you know full well you will receive an inheritance from him as your reward.*[1]

1. Col. 3:23-24 (second reading)

## Visitation
## (May 31)

Read Lk. 1:39-56

> *...who am I that the mother of my Lord should come to me?*[1]

And she does! When I prayerfully look to you, Mary, as Mother of my Lord—and Mother given to me—you bring Him to me, reveal Him to me. In some manner you facilitate His being born in me, through love. You are "Mother of pure love": Mother of the Lord, who is God, who is Love.

But help me, Mother. Why should I be honored with a visit from *my Lord?* In the holy sacrament He comes to me, "He who is"—and there is nothing apart from Him—true God of true God. He who is infinity of perfect Being comes to this micro-being so flawed.

Teach me, Mother, never to cease singing with wonder as your heart sang,

> *My being proclaims the greatness of the Lord,*
> *my spirit finds joy in God my Savior....*
> *God who is mighty has done great things for me....*[2]

Let me never cease thanking the Lord who gives me faith to believe this, even of myself; who gives me grace sometimes to feel it, to be certain of it.

> *His mercy is from age to age.*[3]

For those who desire, those who are hungry. May I always be hungry. And always acknowledge my poverty, that He may graciously enrich me.

*The hungry he has given every good thing,*
*while the rich he has sent empty away.*[4]

Holy Mother, let me not sit smugly enjoying the great things He has done for me, in miserly fashion counting my riches. Like you, I must go quickly to the rough country, and offer my services to my cousins, my brothers who have need, and to share with them the joy of what God has done for every one of us.

1. Lk. 1:43
2. Lk. 1:46-47, 49
3. Lk. 1:50
4. Lk. 1:53

## Immaculate Heart of Mary (Saturday Following Second Sunday After Pentecost)

*I am the Mother of pure love, of fear,*
*of knowledge, and of holy hope.*[1]

Mother of pure love!
From your heart the white flame
flaring out
to flake and blow off
my own heart's wild weedstems,
sweep the soot of smoking desires.

Pure love:
Soft sunlight out of clean blue.
Steady lamp lighted
by Trinity's sacred flame,
illuminating Wisdom's work,
limning the unseeable,
outlining the limitless,
spotlighting presence of God.

Mother of holy hope—
Mistress of fear—
guiding star at sea,
buoy at the reef,
lighthouse looking to port.

Mother of Christ,
with spark from the Holy Spirit
you have lit the Light of the world.

1. Addition by some authorities to Sir. 24:17, and formerly used in the liturgy of the Blessed Virgin. Omitted in the N.A.B.

## Transfiguration
## (August 6)

Read Mk. 9:2-10
2 Pt. 1:16-19

### I Glory

Jesus led Peter, James and John up a high mountain.

> *He was transfigured before their eyes and his clothes became dazzlingly white—whiter than the work of any bleacher could make them. Elijah appeared to them along with Moses; the two were in conversation with Jesus.*[1]

We who follow Christ like the disciples need very much to see the balanced picture of His glory and His sufferings and death. In our own lives there must be occasions of exaltation and spiritual joy as there will certainly be times of depression, sorrow and humiliation. In a faith-companionship with Christ there will be those happy moments when like Peter we will say, *how good it is for us to be here!*

The disciples shared a preview of glory which would be their full vision and possession only after Jesus had finished His redeeming mission, and they had finished their own life's mission. In Moses and Elijah here with Jesus, a glorious confirmation was given the Law and the prophets, fulfilled in the Messiah.

> *...out of the cloud a voice, "This is my Son, my beloved. Listen to him."*[2]

We still have a Law to accept and observe, but the Law as Jesus simplified and sublimated it. And the prophets are still useful towards knowledge and hope, as we read in the letter of Peter:

> *...we possess the prophetic message as something altogether reliable. Keep your attention closely fixed on it, as you would on a lamp shining in a dark place until the first streaks of dawn appear and the morning star rises in your hearts.*[3]

Our faith continually struggles to harmonize concepts hopelessly at variance, Jesus as both God and man. He presents Himself as the Suffering Servant of Isaiah and as the Son of Man of Daniel. In the latter we see the Son of Man receiving from the Father His right to the loyalty of all men:

> *When he reached the ancient One*
> *and was presented before him,*
> *He received dominion, glory, and kingship....*[4]

## II Through Death

In the Lucan account, when Moses and Elijah appeared with Jesus in glory they were speaking of the death which He was to "accomplish" in the Holy City. When the vision ended and they were returning, Jesus asked them not to speak of it until after His resurrection from the dead.[5] Humiliation and glorification, death and resurrection, are together the Christian message. Until faith gives power for the human mind to leap the barriers built by universal experience, "resurrection" is incomprehensible. In puzzlement, the three apostles *continued to discuss what "to rise from the dead" meant.*[6]

After the ascension Paul would find that this fundamental of the Christian message was also a chief obstacle to its complete acceptance. At Athens he was preaching that God is calling all men to repentance, that He has appointed Jesus to be judge of all.

> *"...one whom he has endorsed in the sight of all by raising him from the dead." When they heard about the raising of the dead, some sneered....*[7]

And before the Roman governor he would say in his defense that his only crime was to start a disturbance when he preached the resurrection of Jesus.

> *"I am on trial before you today because of the resurrection of the dead."*[8]

"Lord, it is wonderful for us to be here," to see Your exaltation, that when we see You suffering and dying we may better understand that glory follows humiliation, life springs from death.

1. Mk. 9:2-4 (Gospel, B)
2. Mk. 9:7
3. 2 Pt. 1:19 (second reading)
4. Dn. 7:13-14 (first reading)
5. Cf. Lk. 9:31 (Gospel, C)
6. Mk. 9:10
7. Acts 17:31-32
8. Acts 24:21

## Assumption of Mary
## (August 15)

Read Rv. 11:19; 12:1-6, 10

### I Sign of the Moon

*A great sign appeared in the sky, a woman clothed with the sun, with the moon under her feet, and on her head a crown of twelve stars.*[1]

In mid-July, 1969, a 363-foot rocket blasted off from Cape Kennedy, projecting three men into moon orbit after three and one-half days of space travel. A strange, bug-like vehicle settled on the hot, dusty surface of the moon. A man, encased in cumbersome and complicated gear, slowly emerged, crawled down a short ladder, and gingerly put a foot upon this utterly new and strange world. An age-old dream of man had come true as he now stood on his first extra-terrestrial body. It was a magnificent feat of human technological science and teamwork. The whole country and much of the world paused from myriad earthly occupations to look up to the heavens through the window of a television set. The lunar landing was a sign of human greatness, and all felt a sharing in it.

But dissident voices arose to question the significance of this "sign of the moon." A civil rights leader says: "A society that can resolve to conquer space; to put man in a place where in ages past it was considered only God could reach; to appropriate vast billions; to systematically set about to discover the necessary scientific knowledge—that society deserves both our acclaim and our contempt. It deserves acclaim for achievement and contempt for bizarre social values. For though it has had the capacity to meet extraordinary challenges, it has failed to use its ability to rid itself of the scourges of racism, poverty and war, all of which were brutally scarring the nation even as it mobilized for the assault on the solar system."[2]

And a philosopher: "It is not the outermost reaches of space, but the innermost recesses of the human soul that now demand our most intense exploration and cultivation.... The prime task of our age is not to conquer space but to overcome the institutionalized irrationalities that have sacrificed the values of life to the expansion of power, in all its demoralizing and dehumanizing forms."[3]

## II Sign From Heaven

The Church offers another sign on the feast of the Assumption of the Mother of Christ,

> *...a great sign...a woman...the moon under her feet.*

This is the sign of a better hope and a richer life. The moon is under her feet, twelve stars crown her head. Christian faith has the audacity to tell us that the greatness of a human person, because of his relation to Christ, exceeds that of the universe in which he appears as an infinitesimal germ of life. The sign of this life, reshaping the earth and reaching into eternity, is primarily the Church, Christ the eternal God-man living in a spiritual unity with men. This is the perennial joy of believers, that man can have life unlimited in Jesus Christ. God so loved the world, this unique planet He created wonderfully superior to the other heavenly bodies, that He came into it.

We specially honor on this feast the Mother through whom God assumed human nature and stepped personally into our world. The Church lovingly applies to Mary the sign proper to herself because she is the Mother of the Church.

Mary is praised as the new and greater Judith who saved her people from their enemies. Mary confronted the powers of spiritual evil. Through her, God saved His people for spiritual, unlimited life.

> *Blessed are you, daughter, by the Most High God, above all the women on earth; and blessed be the Lord God, the Creator of heaven and earth, who guided your blow at the head of the chief of our enemies.*
>
> *You are the glory of Jerusalem,*
> *the surpassing joy of Israel;*
> *You are the splendid boast of our people....*[4]

1. Rv. 12:1 (first reading)
2. Ralph David Abernathy, *Newsweek* (7-7-69), p. 60
3. Lewis Mumford, *Newsweek* (7-7-69), p. 61
(2, 3—Copyright *Newsweek*, Inc., 1969, reprinted by permission.)
4. Jdt. 13:18; 15:9

# All Saints
(November 1)

Read Rv. 7:2-4, 9-14
Mt. 5:1-12

## I Community of Perfect Love

Through the year the Church honors certain saints as persons whose lives have highlighted some particular aspect of the human perfection resulting from love of God and man. The number thus honored liturgically must remain small. Today's feast honors *all* the saints, the one great family now sharing the happiness of God their Father, in a perfect community of love.

Here are all the truly great men and women who ever walked the earth, from the beginning of human existence. They are the *chosen,*

> *a huge crowd which no one could count from every nation and race, people and tongue.*

They are the *victorious,*

> *dressed in long white robes and holding palm branches in their hands.... "These are the ones who have survived the great period of trial...."*[1]

In the second reading we are reminded that we on earth are already joined to this community of love by our call to be God's children. We cannot fathom the joy of heaven, but the clear vision of God "as he really is" will elicit a transporting and transfiguring response of love in union.

*Dearly beloved,*
*we are God's children now;*
*what we shall later be has not yet come to light.*
*We know that when it comes to light*
*we shall be like him,*
*for we shall see him as he is.*[2]

## II The Absent

We will not find here many who seemed great and enviable:

Not the rich who trusted in their wealth and left the desire of heavenly joys to men who had not those of earth. Nor those who envied the rich, and spent their lives trying to become so.

*Blest are you poor; the reign of God is yours....*
*But woe to you rich, for your consolation is now.*[3]

Not the self-sufficient and strong-armed who pushed aside the weak, used others for their own purposes, and reveled in power and success.

*How blest are the poor in spirit:*
*the reign of God is theirs.*[4]

Not they with the hollow laugh and defiant sneer, who plucked all the delights of life where they found them and never knew remorse for their thefts; who searched not for justice but self-satisfaction.

*Woe to you who laugh now; you shall weep in your grief.*[5]
*Blest are they who hunger and thirst for holiness; they shall have their fill.*[6]

Not the quarreling and turbulent who matched love of self with contempt for others; who rejected conciliation as demeaning and compromise as weakness.

*Blest, too, the peacemakers; they shall be called sons of God.*[7]

## III Festival

Among the saints we honor are many of our own relatives and friends. And could it not be that one of the delightful surprises awaiting us as we eventually join them will be gratitude from some whom we, all unawares, had helped by our actions or prayers?

"Let us all rejoice in the Lord, celebrating a festival day in honor of all the saints."[8]

Rejoice in the glory of these our friends, in their perfect, unalterable happiness, in the honor and beauty which is their inheritance, in their special bliss which is the vision of God, in their prayers for the People of God, in so many ways distressed and suffering.

Celebrate the glory given to God by these the greatest and noblest of the race, who make amends for sin and dishonor to Him.

*"Praise and glory, wisdom and thanksgiving and honor, power and might, to our God forever and ever. Amen!"*[9]

"I believe...in the communion of saints...and life everlasting."[10]

1. Rv. 7:9, 14 (first reading)
2. 1 Jn. 3:2
3. Lk. 6:20, 24
4. Mt. 5:3
5. Lk. 6:25
6. Mt. 5:6 (Gospel)
7. Mt. 5:9
8. Entrance antiphon
9. Rv. 7:12
10. Apostles' Creed

## All Souls
## (November 2)

*Be on guard, therefore. The Son of Man will come when you least expect him.*[1]

*...he is near, standing at your door.*[2]

How will my heart speak, O God, when the footfall of Your angel of death is heard approaching? At times I hear his tread, but there is no judging of the distance. It is one of Your mercies, Lord, that we cannot know the time of his arrival; that the *time* of it is just as uncertain as the *fact* of it is certain.

Death, O God, is such a common thing, daily recorded, multiplied on Your earth every minute. But You know how singular and momentous it will be to *me*, when it is my *personal* experience. How very *un*common: sharing in importance Your creative act that brought me out of nothingness, made me to *be*. We seem insignificant in a teeming world, a small bead in the endless chain of life. Yet how precious is each human person to You—this *me*, individual, unique, and redeemed by the death of Your Son.

Death brings judgment. You will ask me to account for the immense disparity between this my life of a son and the life of Your only-begotten, eternal Son. This prospect strips away all self-confidence.

You have said, Lord Jesus, that love is what matters. Your chosen Peter sinned grievously, but dared to say, *Lord, you know everything. You know well that I love you.*[3] I also will dare to say, "You know I love You"—not really well, not constantly, not generously, but I do love You.

And You have said, *When you have done all you have been commanded to do, say, 'We are useless servants. We have done no more than our duty.'*[4] I know that I have not done all I have been told to do. But Your mercy embraced the extortionist tax collector, Magdalene, a thief dying on a cross. So I will trust Your heart. I shall await the knock of Your messenger with sorrow more than fear, with regret more than anxiety, and with Your great gift of faith suppressing natural trepidation.

Surely, O God, this is a time for gratitude, the ending of a life that could hold such an expanse of blessings. You delighted me with all Your magnificent creation: the limitless grandeur of the starry heavens; the hidden perfection of a snowflake, an insect's wing; the mysterious beauty of a silent, snowed-in fir forest on a mountain; the song of a carefree child at play. And the ingenious creation of an architect or artist; the unsensed perfection of human goodness, sacrifice and love.

It is here, O heart of my Lord, on love, that I pause and look back with both gratitude and regret. Grateful that I have received so much love from others and above all from You; regretful that I have not better reflected Your own love after having so often shared the sacrament of unity and love.

Like all men, surely, at the end, I will desire to have a legacy for all the loved ones, friends, benefactors, relatives, all brothers and sisters in Christ. I would pray that *You,* O God—since *I* have empty hands—would give them this, *only* this, if You will, but *all* of this: to know You, O infinite good, to love You, O infinite Love.

Death is the punishment of sin. We accept it, as the payment of sin's last debt. Even to the Christian, though, it is a dark passage. But we grasp with firm hand our candle of faith and go forward trustingly into the shadows, even with a song:

Light of Christ!
Thanks be to God!

1. Lk. 12:40
2. Mt. 24:33
3. Jn. 21:17
4. Lk. 17:10

## Immaculate Conception of Mary (December 8)

Read Eph. 1:3-6, 11-12
Lk. 1:26-35

### I Making of a Mother

In the thought of God, Creator of the universe, all things are present. Of all His works, the humanity of Christ is greatest. Because of His divine nature, Christ is Alpha and Omega, Beginning and End. To Him all creation converges, to glorify the Creator.

> *He is the image of the invisible God, the first-born of all creatures. In him everything in heaven and on earth was created, things visible and invisible...all were created through him, and for him. He is before all else that is. In him everything continues in being.*[1]

But He was to be born of a woman, be like us in all but sin, share our human nature. So a mother was prepared. In this Advent feast we rejoice in the way God prepared that mother. We who have come to know and love her can pray, simply and joyfully, by being glad for her joy, her gifts and prerogatives.

We were present to God, were loved, even before we actually existed.

> *God chose us in him before the world began...; he likewise predestined us through Christ Jesus to be his adopted sons....*[2]

And if we, how much more is Mary chosen, graced:

*The Lord begot me, the first-born of his ways,*
*the forerunner of his prodigies of long ago;*
*From of old I was poured forth,*
*at the first, before the earth.*[3]

*I rejoice heartily in the Lord,*
*in my God is the joy of my soul;*
*For he has clothed me with a robe of salvation...*
*like a bride bedecked with her jewels.*[4]

In this choice by God of a woman to bring divinity to humanity, all womanhood is exalted.

In this preparation of a Mother, Mary, conceived without our common stain, clothed with integrity from her conception, is the cue for the entrance of the Holy One of God.

Mary, ever virgin: in this unique arrangement for the conception and birth of Christ into our world is a hint of the value of celibacy in those who aspire to a special role and effectiveness in bringing Christ to men.

## II Building of a Temple

*Wisdom has built her house,*
*she has set up her seven columns....*[5]

Christ, presented in the New Testament as Word and Wisdom, has built a house, a temple, for Himself. Seven columns uphold it:

Faith, hope, love,
prudence, temperance, justice, fortitude.

In no other building of God are there columns so perfectly matched and polished; or superstructure so exquisitely proportioned and detailed. This is a jewel standing sharply sculptured by sun and shadow of God's Providence.

> *"How awesome is this shrine! This is nothing else than an abode of God, and that is the gateway to heaven!"*[6]
>
> "Glorious things are said of you, O Mary,
> because he who is mighty has done great things
> for you."[7]
>
> *"My being proclaims the greatness of the Lord,
> my spirit finds joy in God my Savior."*[8]
>
> Rejoice, Mary, so highly favored! And pray for us your children.

1. Col. 1:15-17
2. Eph. 1:4-5 (second reading)
3. Prv. 8:22-23 (Common Blessed Virgin Mary, first reading, n. 5)
4. Is. 61:10 (entrance antiphon)
5. Prv. 9:1
6. Gn. 28:17
7. Communion antiphon
8. Lk. 1:46-47

## On Life and Death

Read Wis. 3:1-9

*The angel then showed me the river of life-giving water, clear as crystal, which issued from the throne of God and of the Lamb....*[1]

Life is a spring:
bedrock-and-earth-born thing,
mingling its small, still flow
with many another, so
that its restless rivulet
grows to a turbulent band—
now strafed by the sand
piled by its own mad play.
Free, yet keeping a way
some law of its life has set.

Speeded by walls,
narrowed, dashed over falls;
then resting under the fronds
in quiet ponds.
But out again, on, to the sea!
For its measure of being must leap
into the Infinite Deep;
leaving all strife,
merging with measureless life,
in peace, for eternity.

*But the souls of the just are in the hand of God....*
*They seemed, in the view of the foolish, to be dead;*
*and their passing away was thought an affliction,*
*and their going forth from us, utter destruction.*
*But they are in peace.*[2]

1. Rv. 22:1
2. Wis. 3:1-3

## In the Autumn of Life: Peace and Joy

As a poet has put it, the name "October" suggests a month "full and round," but with shortened days and the fading of summer's vigorous, expansive life. There is the quiet brooding, mellowness and tranquility of age, and a mixture of happy summer remembrance and vague regret, of misty melancholy, and bold revelry of blazing sunlit foliage. After the intense leafing, blossoming growth of spring, and the maturing in summer's heat and storms, the aging year reveals a fruitfulness that was partly hidden under luxuriance of leaf and vine. It does not stagger to death in dark despair, but breaks out in a wildly colorful revelry in defiance of death.

What is the mystery of this mad celebration in the face of the approaching season of barren, frozen silence? Everywhere in the woodland's variations of brilliant colors and subdued shades we find the red of the blood of Christ. Splashed fresh on the still-green leaves of the red oak, hanging in large bright drops of berry and crab apple, dried on the burgundy leaves of the viburnums and red-browns of white oak, burning like fire in the euonymus. In the maple's scarlet and orange, the blood red is charged with the glowing gold of the love of the royal heart which redeemed us by the shedding of blood.

This redemption has made tolerable the steady approach of the winter of death; it has colored the autumn of life with festive beauty, filled it with soaring hope. Though the trees will soon stand as dark skeletons against the gray heavens, and lifeless stalks will be gently covered with the cold mantle of snow, nature's pall is white, and promises resurrection, another spring and newness of life.

> *The seed you sow does not germinate unless it dies.... What is sown in the earth is subject to decay, what rises is incorruptible.*[1]

1. 1 Cor. 15:36, 42

## A Closing Prayer

A closing prayer: for the end of a day; of a period, a happy experience; of a trial or crisis; and especially for the end of a life based on faith.

*I will give thanks to you, O Lord my God,*
*with all my heart,*
*and I will glorify your name forever.*
*Great has been your kindness toward me....*

Ps. 86:12-13

# INDEX OF SUBJECTS

## Daughters of St. Paul

**In Massachusetts**

50 St. Paul's Avenue, *Boston,* Mass. 02130
172 Tremont Street, *Boston,* Mass. 02111

**In New York**

78 Fort Place, *Staten Island,* N.Y. 10301
625 East 187th Street, *Bronx,* N.Y. 10458
525 Main Street, *Buffalo,* N.Y. 14203

**In Connecticut**

202 Fairfield Avenue, *Bridgeport,* Conn. 06603

**In Ohio**

2105 Ontario St. (at Prospect Ave.), *Cleveland,* Ohio 44115

**In Pennsylvania**

1127 South Broad Street, *Philadelphia,* Pa. 19147

**In Florida**

2700 Biscayne Blvd., *Miami,* Florida 33137

**In Louisiana**

4403 Veterans Memorial Blvd., Metairie, *New Orleans,* La. 70002
86 Bolton Avenue, *Alexandria,* La. 71301

**In Missouri**

203 Tenth St. (at Pine), *St. Louis,* Mo. 63101

**In Texas**

114 East Main Plaza, *San Antonio,* Texas 78205

**In California**

1570 Fifth Avenue, *San Diego,* Calif. 92101
278 17th Street, *Oakland,* Calif. 94612
46 Geary Street, *San Francisco,* Calif. 94108

**In Canada**

3022 Dufferin Street, *Toronto* 395, Ontario, Canada

**In England**

57, Kensington Church Street, *London* W. 8, England

**In Australia**

58, Abbotsford Rd., Homebush, N.S.W., *Sydney* 2140, Australia